Prophets
AND PERSONAL
Prophecy

BOOKS BY DR. BILL HAMON

Apostles, Prophets, and the Coming Moves of God

The Day of the Saints

The Eternal Church

Personal Prophecy Series

Prophets and the Prophetic Movement II

Prophets, Pitfalls, and Principles III

Prophetic Scriptures Yet to Be Fulfilled

Who Am I and Why Am I Here?

AVAILABLE FROM DESTINY IMAGE PUBLISHERS

Prophets AND Personal Prophecy

God's Prophetic Voice Today

Guidelines for Receiving, Understanding, and Fulfilling God's Personal Word to You

Dr. Bill Hamon

Destiny Image® Publishers, Inc.
P.O. Box 310, Shippensburg, PA 17257-0310

"Speaking to the Purposes of God for This Generation and for the Generations to Come."

Printed in the U.S.A.

This book and all other Destiny Image, Revival Press, MercyPlace, Fresh Bread, Destiny Image Fiction, and Treasure House books are available at Christian bookstores and distributors worldwide.

For a U.S. bookstore nearest you, call 1-800-722-6774.

For more information on foreign distributors, call 717-532-3040.

Or reach us on the Internet: www.destinyimage.com.

For Worldwide Distribution

Trade Paper ISBN: 978-0-7684-3261-9
Hardcover ISBN: 978-0-7684-3473-6
Large Print ISBN: 978-0-7684-3474-3
Ebook ISBN: 978-0-7684-9104-3

1 2 3 4 5 6 7 8 9 10 / 15 14 13 12 11 10

DEDICATION

This book is dedicated to the great company of prophets whom God is raising up in these last days, to the multitude of Christians who have heard the voice of God and want to fulfill His personal word to them, and to those pastors and Christian leaders who need guidelines for counseling people about prophets and personal prophecy.

APPRECIATION

Heartfelt appreciation is given to my wife, Evelyn, for her encouragement for me to finish the book and her willingness to play second fiddle to the book until it was finished, to the Christian International staff for carrying on the CI ministry while their president was writing, and to those obedient vessels who kept prophesying the book to be written. Special appreciation is given to Paul Thigpen for his dedicated, donated, professional editing in appreciation of the prophet and personal prophecy.

CAPITALIZATION

Dr. Hamon has taken Author's Prerogative in capitalizing certain words that are not usually capitalized according to the standard grammatical practice. This is done for the purpose of clarity and emphasis. References to the Church/Bride are capitalized because of her union with Deity through Jesus Christ. Prophets are put in bold in chapter two for emphasis.

All scriptures are taken from the King James Version (KJV) except when designated.

COMMENDATIONS

C. PETER WAGNER, Chancellor—Wagner Leadership Institute

One of the principal figures whom God has been using to shape this generation of believers is my friend, Bishop Bill Hamon. I must confess that I still feel a sense of awe when I call Bill Hamon a "friend." For years and years he was, for me, a distant Christian celebrity, whose name I knew and heard frequently, whom I greatly admired, and whose books had been among the most influential in nurturing me through what I refer to as my "paradigm shift" from traditional Christianity to an openness to the person and to the full ministry of the Holy Spirit. I never was presumptuous enough to imagine that I would ever meet him personally, much less develop the strong relationship that we now have.

JOHN GIMENEZ, Apostle—Rock Church International

Finally, a book that will help saints understand their personal word from God. It should save pastors hours of counseling time. This book is not an abstract doctrinal presentation but a practical "how-to" guide on what personal prophecy is and what you are supposed to do with it. This book is an absolute must for anyone who has ever heard (or thought they heard) from God.

EMANUELE CANNISTRACI, Founder— Evangel Christian Fellowship

The greatest and most complete presentation on personal prophecy ever written. Millions of Christians believe that God has communicated with them and that the Holy Spirit has directed them. The guidelines given in this book for recognizing and relating to a true word from the Lord are a must for those desiring spiritual maturity.

KEN SUMRALL, Founder—Church Foundational Network

A thorough and balanced presentation of the office of the prophet and personal prophecy. Dr. Hamon speaks not from theory, but as a recognized prophet with experiential knowledge of the prophetic ministry. I heartily recommend this valuable book for study for every believer.

GARY GREENWALD, Apostle—Eagles Nest Ministry

Dr. Bill Hamon is one of the most mature and accurate prophets in the Church today. His prophetic ministry flows with divine love and wisdom. He is a forerunner and father to many in the company of prophets today. The prophesying of the prophets will bring the Church from a scattered valley of dry bones to a unified exceeding great army of the Lord (Ezek. 37).

NORVEL HAYES, Founder—Norvel Hayes Minstries & New Life Bible Church

Titus 2:1 says to speak things which become the teaching that is healthy. Specific guidelines are needed for the prophetic ministry to be healthy. Prophets and Personal Prophecy is a valid ministry in the Church today. A New Testament church has to have the different ascension offices and gifts of the Holy Spirit operating. A church that never has a prophet or any of the other fivefold ministries, will always be crippled and weak. It may be a nicely growing church but it will always be spiritually weak.

JIM JACKSON, President—Christian Believers United

Recognizing the tremendous need for clarity and understanding the role of the prophet within the Church today, along with the need for this role to be fulfilled, it is my privilege to recommend this timely and significant book. We live in a day in which we are desperate for the pure word of God, as heard through His anointed prophets, in order that we may receive direction, correction, and edification to more effectively serve our Lord and Savior, Jesus Christ.

Dr. Bill Hamon is truly one of God's special men who have been given a transparent understanding of the role of the prophet. He is being used through a great anointing as a prophet himself. By the power of the Holy Spirit, he is personally responsible for activating hundreds of others through the release and impartation of this gift.

As President of Christian Believers United, and Executive Director of the National Leadership Conference, it has been my privilege to direct and host hundreds of conferences on Christian growth for the equipping of the saints of God for service. Our speakers and teachers have included, along with Bill Hamon, such distinguished men and women of God as Jamie Buckingham, Kenneth Copeland, John and Anne Gimenez, Jack Hayford, Derek Prince, Oral Roberts, Ken Sumrall, and Iverna Tompkins. Dr. Hamon is in that company of speakers most requested by those truly serious about knowing God's agenda for their lives. Dr. Hamon is an instrument of blessing and encouragement as a key speaker and teacher at conferences throughout the world.

This significant book enhances the effectiveness of Dr. Hamon's Ministry and imparts to every student of the Bible an in-depth respect, knowledge, and revelation about today's anointed prophets and their validity. As God's own people, we are awakened to the prophets' value and importance for each individual as well as the Church at large.

Few people in ministry today have had, for me, the personal impact of Dr. Bill Hamon. He is both a co-laborer in Christ and a close friend. I have grown to respect him as an anointed, effective man and prophet of God.

I know this book will prove to be an important resource manual for all God's people. It is ideal for personal study or as a text for the classroom. *Prophets and Personal Prophecy* should become required reading for every Christian leader and believer. You will be enlightened and enriched as you read this book and as you apply to your own life the principles it contains.

CONTENTS

Self-image and Soul-blockage Hindrances

Impatience Produces an "Ishmael" Ministry

Misapplication and Misinterpretation
of Prophecy

Blame Shifting, Self-discipline, and
People Pleasing

Hindrances From Four Types of Human Soil

Proper Principles for Prophesying

Problem of Prophesying From *Logos* Doctrine

Presumptuous Personal Prophecies
Produce Problems

Walking in the Word and Moving in
the Spirit

Prophets and Personal Prophecy to Purify
and Prepare

Spiritual Maturity: No Longer
Privilege—Now Priority

Foreword

by

Oral Roberts

Bill Hamon, A Prophet For Our Time

I always take notice when Bill Hamon prophesies or writes a book on prophetic truths, or even if I'm just with him in prayer and discussion.

Bill's life in Jesus and Jesus' working His prophetic spirit through him, shows to the world—and the Body of Christ—that it's time we realized God has set in the Church not only pastors, evangelists, and teachers, but also apostles and prophets (Eph. 4:11).

I've known for a long time any of us who are "set in the Church" as a pastor, evangelist, teacher, prophet, or apostle, operate under the apostolic and prophetic spirit of the Holy Spirit. Also at any time, anyone in one or more of these offices of the ministry can manifest the spirit of apostle or prophet. In other words, the apostolic and prophetic covering is over all five offices. However, I also know there is a distinct office of each of these five, including that of the prophet.

To see Bill Hamon operating in the prophetic office, to see his humble spirit of giving God all the glory and his carefulness to line up all he says and does with the Word of God, is a blessing that I need, and, I believe, all the people of God need.

God bless Bill's new book, *Prophets and Personal Prophecy*, to all who are blessed to read and study it. I thank God we are living in the days when God is placing a fresh, new emphasis on all the five offices of His Body, including that of the apostle and prophet.

PREFACE

Bill Hamon's religious background can best be described as "American heathen." In his early years, neither his parents, nor any of his four brothers and sisters, were churchgoers. Living out on a 160-acre farm in rural Oklahoma, he had never even set foot inside a church building. But all that changed on July 29, 1950—his sixteenth birthday.

Bill had been attending a Brush Arbor meeting for four weeks in the countryside of southeastern Oklahoma. That night, he accepted Christ Jesus as his personal Savior as he knelt by his bedside at home. Two nights later he walked down the old "sawdust trail" between bridge planks laid across some logs cut from the surrounding trees. Electricity had not yet been brought to that part of the community, so kerosene lanterns were hanging from the poles that held up the brush laid across the top. An accordion and some guitars were playing while the saints were singing the invitational songs.

As he reached the front, Bill knelt at that old rustic bridge board altar and started praying. Within a few moments he was gloriously filled with the Holy Spirit and began speaking in a heavenly language.

Bill had to begin and continue his Christian walk for several years before any of the rest of his family would become

Christians. He was the firstfruits, but within the next ten years he would lead all of his family to the Lord except his older brother, who became a Christian while Bill was in Bible college. After graduating from high school, Bill moved away from home and started living on his own in a boarding house in Amarillo, Texas, and began attending an Independent Restorational church. In October of 1952, he had just finished reading a book proclaiming that one could have power with God through prayer and fasting. The book's emphasis on the value of fasting, and his own zeal for God, motivated him to fast for seven days. He had a burning desire to be all that God would want and allow him to become.

At the end of the seven-day fast, Bill was still crying out to know God's plan for his life. This was such a serious, traumatic time of his life that his heartrending cries were written down, hoping that someday he would understand why he was feeling and thinking as he did. On February 3, 1953, Bill wrote:

> *I am going to describe the way I feel and the thoughts that keep coming to my mind since fasting and praying about what the Lord Jesus would have me to do. When I pray, I feel that the Lord Jesus has called me to the ministry, but again, I don't know for sure. I want to know some certain way whether He has called me or not.*

> *Sometimes I get so confused, discouraged, and downhearted that I just don't know what to do. There is something within that makes me want to go out in the ministry and work for God; then comes that uncertainty about whether it is the Lord's will or not. But even if it were revealed to be His will, how would I ever become a minister? I don't know how you get into the ministry. So why do the thoughts about being a minister keep coming to me?*

> *I can pray, but it doesn't seem like I can get a definite answer. Sometimes I feel like just forgetting about the ministry, or trying to tell myself that I am not called to preach. Maybe I should just go on and serve the*

Lord and not worry about whether I am called to preach or not.

But then hunger wells up within my heart, with a great desire to preach God's Word and work for Him. It makes me feel very sad and depressed to think that God may not have called me to do some kind of work for Him. I guess only time will tell, and patience to wait before the Lord. I know what I desire, but I have no idea how to fulfill that desire, or whether God even wants it fulfilled.

To answer his questions, this young man did not receive an angelic visitation, a voice from Heaven, or a dream. Instead, God sent a prophet with a personal word of prophecy for him. Bill himself had been used by God several times to speak out in the assembly with prophetic utterances, but he had never seen a manifestation of personal prophecy to an individual before. So he was a bit surprised when the prophet laid hands on him and prophesied:

For, yea, saith the Lord, you shall grow tall and broad in the Lord. You shall testify to those of your own age and they shall call you off to a separate place, desiring to know the Word of God. You shall wait upon the Lord and He shall give you revelations of His Word. For yea, you shall see dreams. The Lord thy God is preparing thee for that work which He has called thee to do and to fulfill His own purpose and pleasure in thee. For the present, remain under the shepherd which you are under, and I will send forth the more mature into the field. I shall send thee forth in My time, saith the Lord. You shall go forth in the eleventh hour, saith God.

At last, he found a glimmer of hope. It was a prophetic word of direction, and encouragement to believe that God had a place for him in His plan and purpose, even as a minister of God in Christ's Church.

This was Bill's first exposure to personal prophecy. He was greatly excited and encouraged, but his analytical, inquisitive mind had many questions. How could this come to pass? He did not have a Christian family heritage, let alone a heritage of ministry. He knew no ministers personally. He had no idea how someone becomes a minister.

Before God speaks to an individual, He already has a plan, a method, and providential circumstances to bring it all to pass in His timing. But this 18-year-old, who had been a Christian less than three years, did not know that God can personally call an individual from youth to do a mighty work for Him in his matured years. So it would be several years before such an understanding and assurance were a part of his faith. All he knew at the time was that he had no idea how all of this could come to pass.

Nevertheless, seven months later, through God's divine providential workings, Bill was attending a Bible college in Portland, Oregon. There, the Lord began teaching this chosen vessel of God about the prophetic ministry, and involving him in it. God wanted him to have a foundation in and an appreciation for the office of the prophet, for personal prophecy, and for the laying on of hands and prophecy by the presbytery. Some 30 years later, Bill would be raised up as a pioneer and a worldwide leader in restoring the office and ministry of the prophet into Christ's Church with full recognition and authority.

No doubt this is the reason God singled him out during that school year as the only young person to be called forth by the faculty to receive prophetic presbytery. It happened this way.

In those early days of the restoration of the prophetic presbytery, no one was called forth to be ministered to unless at least two things happened. First, God had to speak specifically and emphatically about which person was to be chosen, and all the prophetic presbytery ministers had to be in agreement. Second, the candidate desiring ministry from the prophetic presbytery had to fast a minimum of three days even to sit in the section from which candidates would be chosen.

One day an announcement was made by the faculty that a prophetic presbytery would be made available to all those who would fast three days. Bill had already been fasting for six days, so he just continued on for three more. At that appointed service, he was called forth and knelt at the chair as five faculty members laid hands upon him and spoke forth these prophetic utterances on Thursday night, October 1, 1953.

Yea, My son, even as the Spirit of the Lord burned in the heart, yea, even in the bones of My servant Jeremiah, even so doth the fire kindle and burn within thy heart. Yea, thou art as a steed that stands ready to be loosened to go forth, for thou hast the message in thy heart and thou hast an eye that is single and thy love to God has been made known through the Spirit of the Lord.

Fear not, My son, the hand of the Lord hath rested upon thee and the mantle of His power has come upon thee. Yea, and thy mouth shall be quick to speak the word of the Lord, and even as thou shalt speak shall the prophetic utterance come forth, that when thou openest thy mouth to declare the word of the Lord, the Spirit of the Lord shall come mightily upon thee, and "thus saith the Lord" shall come forth. Yea, I give unto thee the word of wisdom and the word of knowledge, yea, and thou shalt see things that eyes have not seen, and thou shalt speak.

Yea, My son, thine heart is filled with the love of thy God and thy God looketh down upon thee, and He will bless thy soul and He will equip thee and yea, thou shalt run quickly, for thine heart is seeking God, and the Lord knoweth thy heart this night. Yea, seek ye the Lord, continue to wait much before Him. For yea, He saith, I will speak to thee in the night hour. I will awaken thee and I will instruct thee and thou shalt open thy mouth and thou shalt speak what the Lord doth speak unto thee. Though thou art young in years, yet My Spirit shall teach thee and thy wisdom shall come forth as the voice of the Lord thy God.

For thus saith the Lord, I have even kept thee unto Mine own purpose. Yea, thou knewest Me not, I even sheltered thee. For lo, thou art a chosen vessel, saith the Lord. Yea, I have chosen thee and appointed thee and thou hast been in the hand of the Lord as an instrument, and now, saith the Spirit, the Lord shall place in thy hands weapons wherewith thou shalt fight. For the Lord shall not send thee forth unprepared, but He shall shield thee with faith and He shall equip thee even with His Spirit.

For lo, as occasion shall serve thee, thou shalt arise and act in faith, for the Lord doth give unto thee faith, even the faith of God. Thou shalt not trust in thine own strength, for thou shall be strengthened with the strength of the Lord thy God. Therefore, fear not, saith the Lord, because of thy youth. Lean thou upon the Lord thy God, for in the hour of crisis He shall sustain thee, and in the hour of danger, He shall not forsake thee.

For thus saith the Lord, thou shalt go forth into every place that I shall send thee, and the word of the Lord shall be in thy mouth. Yea, saith the Lord, a winner of souls shalt thou be, for compassion shall dwell in thee and because of the compassion that is in thine heart, thy faith shall even go forth to challenge the enemy. For demons shall retreat before thee and satan shall yield to thy prayer. For lo, the faith that worketh by love shall work mightily in thee, for to this end hast thou been called, saith the Lord.

Yea, My son, the Spirit of revelation in the knowledge of thy God shall rest upon thee mightily, and behold, the word of the Lord shall flow from thy lips like fresh oil, saith thy God. And yea, thou shalt wield the sword of the Lord fearlessly. Truly I do put deliverance in thy hands, saith the Lord. Truly thou shalt have a ministry of deliverance unto the captives. Truly thou shalt have a ministry of calling My people out, saith the Lord, and for bringing My people together into the one Body, saith

*the Lord. For truly My hand is upon thee that thou
mayest lift up thy voice, even as a trumpet unto My
people, saith the Lord. Truly as the word of the Lord
doth minister through thee by revelation My sheep
shall hear My voice, saith the Lord, and see that lo, the
Master calleth them.*

*Yea, is not this the day of the Lord that He hath
proclaimed? Yea, is not this the day wherein the Lord
thy God shall come unto thee? Yea, is not this the day
that thou shalt go forth in His might and His power?
Have I not said in My Word concerning My own
children, "Ye are gods," and yea in these last days ye
shall go forth as gods? Thou shalt go forth as gods with
power in thine hands, and minister life and faith unto
those that are desolate. Yea, I say unto thee, thou shalt
be a leader of leaders. Yea, thou shalt see multitudes
running unto thee, for as a light upon a tall hill shalt
thou be. Yea, fear shall be in the hearts of those round
about thee, yet thou shalt stand as one full of courage,
saith the Lord.*

On February 4—the following year—Bill was ordained to
the ministry and began pastoring his first church at the age of
19. Only a year before he had been in a dilemma as to whether
God had called him, and if so, how God could get him into the
ministry. But now, through the prophetic word, God's call and
ordination had been confirmed, and he had been confirmed,
and he had been activated and placed in ministry.

Two years later, Bill married a young lady in his church,
Evelyn Hixson. I was that lady, and I became a pastor's wife
at 18. We were blessed in the following six years with two sons
and a daughter.

Meanwhile, God foreknew the ultimate ministry He had
ordained for His chosen vessel, so He made sure Bill received
throughout his years of ministry a maximum exposure to all
restored truth, and experience in all the fivefold ministries. He
pastored six years, evangelized three years, taught in a Bible

college five years, and founded and developed the Christian International undergraduate and graduate School of Theology, which now has an enrollment of over four thousand students, with graduates serving in the ministry all over the world. Bill began the School of the Holy Spirit in 1979, and started prophets conferences and seminars throughout the U.S. and many foreign countries in 1982. He established the School of Prophets for training those called to the prophetic ministry. During these years he continued his own theological education, earning a Master of Theology, and later a national university honored him with a Doctor of Divinity degree in 1973.

It has now been 35 years since Bill began prophesying, received his first personal prophecy from a prophet, received laying on of hands and prophecy by the prophetic presbytery, and received laying on of hands and ordination by a ministerial presbytery. During these nearly four decades, he has laid hands on and personally prophesied over more than fifteen thousand people. These range from small infants to international church leaders, from farmers to politicians, and professional people of all types.

Because of this constant giving, Bill has also reaped in like kind: He has received from others a multitude of personal prophecies. Those that were recorded have all been typed and placed in a five-inch ring notebook, which contains over six hundred pages of double- and single-spaced text. They amount to over 150,000 prophetic words given to the two of us.

These words were prophesied by ministers representing all fivefold ascension gift ministries; by new converts; and ministers who have been ordained over fifty years; by male and female; old and young. They have been received while ministering on almost every continent of the world, from all areas of Christendom where the Holy Spirit is given freedom to express His thoughts to individuals. They have come from Christians in charismatic denominational churches, classical Pentecostal churches, and different "camps" and fellowships such as those called by the names "restoration," "charismatic," "faith," and "kingdom." They have even come from Christian men's and women's organizations such as the Full Gospel Businessmen's Fellowship International and Ladies' Aglow; and from special ministry groups such as Teen Challenge and Maranatha Ministries.

The amazing thing is that in all of these thousands of prophetic words through hundreds of people from all over the world over a period of 35 years, there has been no contradiction spoken to Bill's office and calling of prophet.

Just within the last five years, about 15 prophecies have been received concerning an apostolic anointing to be added to the ascension gift office of the prophet. The Holy Spirit said that this has been given for the purpose of pioneering, establishing, and taking a fatherhood responsibility for the restoration and propagation of the office of the prophet. So Bill understandably has had a burden for writing about the prophet and all levels and realms of the prophetic ministry. This book will be the first of several.

As you read, you will realize that the truths and principles presented in this volume are not just from book learning and research. It includes as well the realities and truths Bill has gleaned on the front line of the prophetic ministry for the last 35 years. These guidelines for receiving, understanding, and fulfilling a true personal word from the Lord are vital for all those who believe that God still speaks to individuals today. I am firmly convinced that no other book has been written that will provide such critical insight and understanding of the nature of personal prophecy. And I pray it will open new doors of ministry and blessing in the lives of all who read it, study it, and apply it faithfully.

Evelyn Hamon

CHAPTER 1

GOD WANTS TO COMMUNICATE

Our God is a personal God. He desires intimate fellowship with individuals more than a distant relationship with humanity as a race. When Adam and Eve were the entire race, the Almighty walked and talked with them. But ever since sin dulled human ears to hearing and human eyes to seeing God, He has not been able to communicate with everyone individually. The race as a whole does not desire His fellowship and is not sensitive enough to hear His voice.

Prophets—God's Communication Channels. For that reason, God has had to find individuals with whom He can communicate personally, and then speak to the rest of the human race through them. Through the ages He has raised up special people called patriarchs and prophets to be His spokesmen to mankind. And in the fullness of time, God spoke to us in the person of Jesus Christ (Heb. 1:1-2), who was God Himself manifest in the flesh (1 Tim. 3:16), the full and complete expression of God Himself (Col. 2:9).

Jesus—God in Human Form. Jesus was Heaven's thoughts, words, principles, plans, and pattern of living made visually and verbally manifest on earth. Though the Old Testament prophets had prophesied in part, often speaking words they themselves did not fully comprehend, Jesus was more than a prophet. He fully understood and expressed His heavenly Father, speaking the whole counsel of God. He was the brightest display of God's glory and the greatest expression of God's personality ever to occur in all eternity.

Jesus thus rent the veil that kept us from seeing God, and removed our dullness of hearing. He made the way for God to come and dwell personally within each individual. When a person is born again by the blood of Jesus and filled with the Holy Spirit, that person's individual body actually becomes a temple of God, a dwelling place for the Most High (1 Cor. 6:19). These individuals are then built together as a spiritual house where the fullness of God can dwell (Eph. 2:19-22).

Jesus—The Prototype of a New Race. This is possible because Jesus the God-Man was the beginning of a whole new race of God-created beings. Christ Jesus was the firstborn among many brethren: the prototype of a whole new creation in Christ who would become like Him, being conformed to His very image and likeness. That human body of Jesus, containing the fullness of the Godhead, was crucified, buried, and resurrected, and as an immortal body it is even now filled with the fullness of God, and the head of multi-millions of redeemed men and women who make up the Church.

The Bible—God in Written Form. After Jesus ascended bodily to Heaven, the world was no longer able to see the fullness of God in the flesh. But Jesus sent us the Holy Spirit, and the Spirit wrote in the Bible the guidelines and standards by which God can be fully known and understood. Rightly understood in its full dimension, the Scripture is sufficient to give us knowledge of all we need to be in our time of mortality and into eternity. The Bible is now the revelation of God, all the sacred writings the mortal Church will ever need to do the whole will of God.

The Prophet—God's Spokesman. Today, through the Bible and the Holy Spirit, God desires to walk and talk with us in an individual, personal, intimate relationship. Yet not all Christians understand how to recognize the voice of the

Lord. Even when they do recognize it, many do not know how to respond to it so that it can be fulfilled. In this way, as in many other ways, no individual is self-sufficient in his relationship with God; we all need the rest of the Body of Christ. So God has set within the Body the ministry of the **prophet** as a special voice; He has established the gift of prophecy as His voice in the midst of the congregation; and He has sent the spirit of prophecy to give testimony of Jesus throughout the world.

Prophecy—The Voice of the Holy Spirit. The coming of the Holy Spirit, the birth of the Church, and the writing of the Bible did not eliminate the need for the prophetic voice of the Lord; in fact, it intensified that need. Peter insisted that the prophet Joel was speaking of the Church age when he proclaimed, "I will pour out My Spirit in those days, and your sons and daughters shall prophesy" (Acts 2:17). Paul emphasized that truth when he told the church at Corinth to "*covet to prophesy*" (1 Cor. 14:39b; see also Eph. 4:11).

God still wants the revelation of His will to be vocalized. So He has established the prophetic ministry as a voice of revelation and illumination that will reveal the mind of Christ to the human race. He also uses this ministry to give specific instructions to individuals concerning His personal will for their lives.

Prophet Ministry—for Illumination, Not Addition. The ministry of the prophet is not, of course, to bring about additions or subtractions to the Bible. Any new additions accepted as infallibly inspired would be counterfeits, false documents that would contain delusions that lead to damnation. Instead, the prophet brings illumination and further specifics about that which has already been written. And the Holy Spirit's gift of prophecy through the saints is to bring edification, exhortation, and comfort to the Church (1 Cor. 14:3).

Personal Prophecy Brings Confirmation and Witness. The Holy Spirit whispering the thoughts of Christ within a Christian's heart is obviously God's divine order for communication. But what the individual has sensed in his spirit must be confirmed: God's counsel is that every word needs to be witnessed to and confirmed in the mouth of two or three witnesses (2 Cor. 13:1). This is a critical role that can be fulfilled by the prophetic voice.

Of course, personal prophecy must never become a substitute for the individual's responsibility and privilege of hearing the voice of God for himself. God is a jealous God, and is not pleased when we allow anything to hinder an intimate relationship and personal communication with Him—even if the hindrance is from a ministry He Himself has ordained. Personal prophecy must not take the place of our duty to fast, pray, and seek God until we hear from Heaven ourselves!

At the same time, many people cannot hear, or will not take time to hear, what God wants to say to them. God is usually more anxious to talk than we are to listen, but He will not always break in on our busy schedules, trying to shout over the noise of the television or social chatter (though occasionally He may catch us while we are asleep). When this is the case, the Lord often uses the voice of the prophet to speak to individuals, congregations, and nations. But His greatest desire is always for His children to take quality time to wait upon Him until our mind, emotions, and will are cleared sufficiently for Him to communicate His heart and mind to us clearly.

Proven Prophetic Principles. For 35 years now I have engaged in prophetic ministry to the Body of Christ. This book, the first in a series on the subject of prophecy, draws on those many years of experience to offer insight for Christians who want to understand more about it. It is not primarily a theological and biblical justification of the authenticity of prophecy in our day; another book will address that issue. Instead, this volume is intended as a practical handbook for those who are already convinced that prophets operate in the Church today, who have themselves received a personal prophecy, and who want to respond properly and fruitfully to what God is saying to them.

Pastoral Counseling Concerning Personal Prophecy. These pages will also serve as a vital resource for those pastors and elders who spend hours counseling people who believe they have received a true word from the Lord. I am aware that even true prophecies, if not rightly understood or responded to, can cause great confusion and wrong decisions among Christians who are immature, uncommitted, or biblically uneducated. How much worse, then, is the havoc created by false prophecies, requiring hours of pastoral counseling to resolve the resulting problems and heal the resulting heartache.

Pastors who face such situations have my sympathy and compassion. I hope that the truths in this book will help them give wise counsel to all those in their congregations who have received personal prophecies. I also hope they will keep in mind that the godly solution to the problems of personal prophecy is not to isolate the saints from it, nor to discourage them from seeking to hear God personally about their specific needs. Instead, the biblical strategy is to train them to discern what is true, and how to respond properly to the true word from the Lord.

The Prophets Are Coming—Prepare! I believe that this is an age in which God is raising up a multitude of prophets who are anointed and appointed—honest, true, trained, and experientially matured. But mixed in among these will be found those prophets who are ignorant, immature, and even false. There will be no place to hide the saints from them in this day of mass media reaching into every home. So the only true salvation from the enemy's falsehoods will be to expose the saints purposefully and properly to true prophets, educate them to discern true from false, and train them in how to respond.

Restoration or Devastation. In God's armory of weapons and means of ministry, few others, I believe, have as great a potential for blessing or devastation as prophecy. Like the laser, it can be used to bring life, healing, and restoration; or confusion, disruption, and death. Prophecy is no play toy. God has not given it merely to satisfy the curious. It is a volatile chemical in God's laboratory that must be handled by experienced hands and used under proper supervision. My prayer is that this book will serve as a laboratory manual for the preparing and equipping of ministers and saints to properly understand prophecy and the ministry of the prophet.

CHAPTER 2

GOD'S PURPOSES FOR PROPHETS

Prophets Are Special to the Heart of God

The **prophetic** ministry is one of the nearest and dearest ministries to the heart of God. The **prophetic** ministry and the voice of the **prophet** were established as God's primary method of communicating with His mankind creation on planet Earth. It was the anointing of the **prophet** upon the patriarchs that enabled Adam, Enoch, Noah, Abraham, Isaac, Jacob, Moses, and others to predict future happenings, to receive instruction from God for new things God wanted to do, to decree the prophetic future of their descendants, to receive revelations from God concerning how to deliver His people from bondage, and to build a tabernacle for God's dwelling. The **prophet** was God's verbal contact with His chosen people. Jehovah did not talk to their king or to the people except through His **prophets**. Almost all of the Old Testament books were written by **prophets**.

Prophets Participate in All of God's Plans and Performances. It was the **prophets** who predicted and prepared the way for the coming of the Messiah. It was a **prophet**, a natural cousin of the Messiah, who prepared the way for the ministry of the Son of God. God reveals His secrets unto His servants, the **prophets**. He reveals by His Spirit the mysteries of His eternal purposes in the Church to His apostles and **prophets**. **Prophets** were a major ministry in the founding of Christ's Church. They were voices giving divine direction to the early Church in its formative years. The office of the **prophet** has been God's voice throughout the Church age to bring repentance to His people and reformation and restoration during divinely predestined "times of refreshing" (Amos 3:7; Eph. 2:19; 3:5; Acts 3:21).

The **prophet** is one of the five gifted ministries that Christ Jesus gave for the perfecting of His saints and the maturing to manhood of His Church. The Book of Revelation declares that the **prophets** are to be instruments of God to execute His judgments. When the seventh angel begins to sound, the mystery of God will be finished, as He has declared to His servants, the **prophets**. The **prophet** and the **prophetic** ministry have been and will continue to be active in every age and dispensation of God's dealings with man. Adam prophesied to his wife in the Garden of Eden before the fall of man. Apostles and **prophets** will be found present at the fall of Babylon, that great and wicked city guilty of shedding the blood of **prophets** and saints (Eph. 4:11-13; Rev. 10:7; 11:10; 18:20).

Prophets Are Special and Precious to God. Yes, **prophets** are very near and dear to the heart of God. They are an integral part of all God is doing on planet Earth. They have not been dispensationally depleted nor cemented into a nonfunctional foundation, but are a vital part of all that God has done and shall ever do in His eternal plan for man. God loves His true **prophets**. He takes special pride and interest in His **prophets**. It is the only ministry of which He makes the emphatic declaration, *"Do My **prophets** no harm."* He who curses one of God's true **prophets** incurs the curse of God. He who blesses a **prophet** in the name of a **prophet** receives the same reward that God gives the **prophet**. *"God hath set some in the Church....**prophets**."* He says, believe His **prophets** and you shall prosper (Ps. 105:15; Matt. 10:41; 1 Cor. 12:28; 2 Chron. 20:20).

God is very sensitive about His **prophets**. To touch one of His **prophets** is to touch the apple of His eye. To reject God's **prophets** is to reject God. To fail to recognize the **prophets**, or to keep them from speaking, is to refuse God permission to speak.

Jesus was a **prophet** in His mortal ministry on earth. He has given that ministry of a **prophet** to men today. Jesus still wants to function as a **prophet** within the Church. To accept and appreciate the ministry of the **prophet** is to accept and appreciate Jesus, the **prophet**. Not to do so is to depreciate that ministry of Jesus to His Church. One reason Jesus is so excited about the restoration of the **prophet** ministry is that it is so near and dear to Him. The restoration of the **prophet** within the Church releases Christ to express Himself more fully to His Church and to the world. Jesus is personally involved in the restoration of the **prophet** to full recognition, position, and ministry (1 Sam. 8:7; Deut. 18:15; Gen. 20:7).

Prophets Prepare the Way for Christ's Second Coming

The **prophet** Malachi prophesied that God would send Elijah the **prophet** before the coming of the great and dreadful day of the Lord (Mal. 4:5). When the angel of the Lord prophesied to Zacharias concerning the birth of John, he used the same thoughts that Malachi prophesied: *"And many of the children of Israel shall he turn to the Lord their God. And he shall go before Him [the Messiah] in the spirit and power of Elias [Elijah], to turn the hearts of the fathers to the children, and the disobedient to the wisdom of the just; **to make ready a people prepared for the Lord**"* (Luke. 1:16-17, emphasis added).

Restoration of Church Prophets a Sign of the Times. It was only natural and according to a literal interpretation of the Scriptures for the Jews to believe that Elijah himself would return personally to prepare the way for the coming of the Messiah. Yet Jesus declared that John the Baptist fulfilled Malachi's prophecy. Jesus stated that John the Baptist was a **prophet**. *"Yea, I say unto you, and more than a **prophet**. For* *this is he, of whom it is written, Behold, I send My messenger before thy face, which shall prepare thy way before thee....And if ye will receive it, this is Elias [Elijah], which was for to come"* (Matt. 11:9b-10,14, emphasis added). John came in the power and spirit of the **prophet** Elijah. Just as one **prophet**, John the Baptist, prepared the way for Christ's first coming, now a **company of prophets** will prepare the way for Christ's second coming. That **company of prophets** is being raised up in the 1980s. God revealed to me that there are ten thousand **prophets** on the North American continent alone being prepared to be released within the Church. This **company of prophets** will come forth in the power and spirit of Elijah. They, as a corporate body of **prophets**, will fulfill the prophecy of Malachi in relation to Christ's second coming as John the Baptist fulfilled it in relation to Christ's first coming. A single **prophet** prepared the way for the Messiah of Israel and Redeemer of mankind. The **company of prophets** will prepare the way for Jesus the King of kings and Lord of lords. The one **prophet** prepared the way for Jesus to come and usher in the Church Age; the many **prophets** will prepare the way for Jesus to come and usher in the Kingdom Age.

Prophets Prepare the Way for Christ's Coming. **Prophets** prepare for Christ's coming in two primary ways. First, they prepare the *way* for the Lord to return. Second, they *make ready a people* prepared for the Lord (Isa. 40:3; Luke 1:17).

How Do Prophets Prepare the Way?

Prophets play a vital role in God's predestined plan for the final return of Christ to the earth. Acts 3:21 declares that the heavens must receive (retain, keep, hold, restrain) *Christ in Heaven until the times of restitution* [restoration] *of all things, which God has spoken by the mouth of all His holy **prophets** since the world began.* There are Old and New Testament prophetic Scriptures that must be fulfilled before Christ can return. The **prophets** have been given the anointing and responsibility to receive from Christ the proper revelation and application of these Scriptures. They are hidden from the eyes of men until God's time for that truth to be restored and established.

New Age Approaching. The Church is now in the beginning days of the transition from the age of the mortal Church to the Kingdom Age. When God was ready to take His people from the dispensation of the Law to the dispensation of the Church, He commissioned His Spirit to bring enlightenment on Scriptures and revelation knowledge concerning the reality and application of that truth. Peter received illumination to perceive that Gentiles could become Christians without becoming Jews first. This was revolutionary revelation knowledge to Peter and all the rest of the apostles. Paul received the revelation knowledge to understand the mystery of the one Body of Christ, the Church. In his letter to the Ephesian church he explained to them that they had been birthed and built upon the foundational ministries of the apostle and **prophet** (Apostle Paul and **Prophet** Silas) with Jesus Christ Himself being the chief cornerstone. They were being built together as a holy temple in the Lord, and as the corporate Body of Christ in order for God to have a habitation and headquarters here on earth. All of this was to be accomplished through the Holy Spirit. This was a revolutionary new concept and a major departure from all that the Jewish theologians had ever taught.

Paul Required to Bring Restoration. Paul justified his teaching not only with Old Testament Scriptures, but also upon the authority of the "Spirit of revelation" and the office anointing of the apostle and **prophet**. He states: *"A dispensation of the grace of God has been given to me for you"* and *"by revelation He made known unto me the mystery of the corporate body of Christ which in other ages was not made known unto the sons of men, as it is **now** revealed unto His holy Apostles and **prophets** by the Spirit"* (Eph. 2:19-22; 3:1-6). Ephesians 3:5 reveals that apostles as well as **prophets** now have the ministry of revealing new truth to the Church.

We are not saying that **prophets** and apostles need to write new Scriptures here in the twentieth century. The

Bible is complete and needs no additions. But the Bible was prophetically inspired, and it requires prophetic Holy Spirit illumination and revelation to understand and apply it rightly. For instance, Martin Luther read the Scripture, *"The just shall live by faith"* and Ephesians 2:8-9 hundreds of times before the Spirit of revelation made known to him the reality of its meaning. When it did dawn upon him, it ushered in the Protestant Reformation. A true revelation always brings a revolutionary change. Martin Luther did not invent or prophesy new Scriptures but received a true revelation about that which had already been written by former apostles and **prophets**.

The same was true for the Holiness Movement, the Pentecostal Movement, and the Charismatic Movement. We are reading Scriptures right now that soon the Holy Spirit will illuminate and activate into full reality. The ascension gift office of the **prophet** has the special anointing for this ministry.

Time for Final "Tidal Wave" Restoration Movement. There have been four major restorational movements during the last 470 years, and several little waves of restorational truths in between. The **company of prophets** will bring revelation and activation of the greatest restorational movement ever recorded. It will be greater than all four previous movements rolled into one. It will be as revolutionary as the change from Judaism to Christianity and from the Dark Ages to the Protestant Reformation. As the final revelations on the last Scriptures to be fulfilled are illuminated and activated it will create a tidal wave of restoration of such proportions that it will fulfill Revelation 11:15 and prepare the way for the second coming of Christ the King Eternal.

The **prophets** prepare the way for the second coming of Christ by bringing revelation knowledge on the Scriptures that must be fulfilled before Christ can return. The Church apostles and **prophets** have been commissioned with that anointing and responsibility. In Revelation 10:7 and 11:15, when the seventh angel has finished sounding, *"The kingdoms of this world are become the kingdoms of our Lord* [Jesus] *and of His Christ* [anointed one—the Church]." *"But in the days of the voice of* *the seventh angel, when he shall begin to sound, the mystery of God should be finished, as He hath declared to His servants the **prophets**."* Nothing will take the Church by surprise as long as God's **prophets** are alive and active in the Church. For *"Surely the Lord God will do nothing, but He revealeth His secret unto His servants the **prophets**"* (Amos 3:7).

Greatest Sign of the Century. The theologians who look to Israel as their signpost for the nearness of the coming of the Lord proclaim the day Israel became a state as the greatest sign of the twentieth century. Those who look to the Church for the signs of the nearness of the coming of the Lord can proclaim the restoration of the **prophet** ministry and the **company of prophets** as the greatest sign of the nearness of His coming in this century. John the Baptist was the greatest sign ever given that the Messiah was at hand, but the religious scribes and Pharisaic theologians could not discern God's greatest sign of the time. Likewise, the majority of denominational ministers will not recognize the greatest sign of the century, the Elijah **company of prophets** that the Holy Spirit is raising up to make the proper preparation for the coming of our King Jesus and His dominion over all the earth. Jesus was already on earth while the **prophet** was preparing the way for His manifestation as the Messiah. The Kingdom of God is already on the earth within the Church awaiting the final revelation of the mystery of God to be finished as revealed by the **prophets**. Yes, the Kingdom of God within the Church is awaiting the final sounding of the trumpet of the seventh angel so that final action can be taken to make the kingdoms of this world the kingdoms of our Lord Jesus Christ. No wonder Jesus is so excited about the restoration of the **prophets**, for they are preparing the way for His return and for His literal Kingdom to be established over all creation (Luke 11:2; 17:21; Rev. 11:15).

Prophets Prepare the Church to Be the Bride of Christ

The **prophets** not only are to prepare the way of the Lord; they are also *"to make ready a people for the Lord."* John the

Baptist could not have fulfilled that prophecy in its entirety, for that "people" is the Church. Peter describes the Church as a people who *were not a people, but are now the people of God," "a peculiar people."* These people are a people who have been purchased by the blood of Jesus. Paul told the elders to *"feed the Church of God, which He hath purchased with His own blood,"* and that *"Jesus loved the Church and gave Himself for the Church that He might present it to Himself a glorious Church, not having spot, or wrinkle, or any such thing, but that it should be holy and without blemish."* His blood cleanses, but it requires the ministry of the **prophet** and the other fivefold ministries *"to make ready a people for the Lord"* (Luke 1:17; 1 Pet. 2:9-10; Acts 20:28; Eph. 5:25-27).

The Church Is the Bride of Christ and must be properly prepared, clothed, and made ready for her wedding day. Jesus is coming for a Bride to enter into a joint-heir reign with Him over all His vast domain. The Church-Bride cannot be an undeveloped little girl or an old wrinkled woman. She must be in the prime of beauty and performance. The Church-Bride must be fully clothed with her wedding garments, which are the garment of salvation, the robe of righteousness, the garment of praise, the armor of God; and fully equipped with her weapons of warfare, which are the gifts of the Holy Spirit. Her sword is the Word of God, which is made sharp by the revelation knowledge provided by the **prophets**.

John described the Bride of Christ as portrayed in the new Jerusalem *"prepared as a bride adorned for her husband,"* and the angel said, *"Come hither, I will shew thee the bride, the Lamb's wife."* Jesus is not marrying a gem city but rather a living body made up of redeemed saints who have been conformed to His own image and likeness. Isaiah prophesied about the Church, the Sons of God, becoming the Bride of Christ. *"For as a young man marrieth a virgin, so shall thy sons marry thee"* (Isa. 62:5a). Hosea prophesied that the day would come when the Lord would betroth His people unto Himself in righteousness and grace. Paul proclaimed to the Corinthian Christians that he had betrothed them to one husband that he might present them as a chaste virgin to Christ (Hos. 2:19-20; 1 Cor. 11:2; Eph. 5:22-33; Rev. 19:7-8; 20:2,9).

The **prophets** are being brought forth to fulfill their part in preparing the Church-Bride for her day of presentation to her heavenly Bridegroom, Christ Jesus. Jesus is rejoicing with great joy over the part the **prophets** are playing in preparing His Bride. When the **prophets** have finished their ministry, He will be released to descend from Heaven with a shout and be fully and eternally united with His Bride. Twentieth-century Church **prophets** are very precious to Christ, for they are perfecting the Bride He died to purchase, the Church. Christ says, woe to those who hinder His true **prophets** from fulfilling their part in preparing His Bride for presentation to Him in perfect purity and maturity. The Church-Bride of Christ cannot be fully perfected without the full restoration of the ministry of the apostles and **prophets** (Eph. 4:11-12).

Prophets Activate Church Members Into Their Membership Ministry. Prophets and the prophetic presbytery have the divinely gifted ability to activate the gifts and talents of the saints and ministers by the laying on of hands and prophecy. They have the ability from God to reveal and confirm those with a call to fivefold ministry. The **prophet** has the ability to reveal to saints their membership ministry in the Body of Christ. This ministry can function while he is a team member with other apostles and **prophets** in a prophetic presbytery or individually in the office of the **prophet**.

The apostle, **prophet**, evangelist, pastor, and teacher were given special ability from Christ to perfect, equip, and mature the saints. Though all five must be able to teach, preach, prophesy, and minister in the gifts of the Holy Spirit, yet each has a special unique anointing and ability that the others do not possess. This book was written to clarify and magnify the office of the **prophet** and the ministry of personal prophecy.

The author does not want the reader to develop the attitude that the **prophet** is more important than the other four. All five are absolutely necessary, anointed, and appointed of

God for the Church. There has been much written about, and a general understanding of, the offices of pastor, evangelist, and teacher. Yet there has been very little written concerning the **prophet**. There is even less acceptance and understanding of twentieth-century Church **prophets**. For these reasons space is only given here to explain the unique ability and anointing of the **prophet**. In relation to our subject, the **prophet** is the one who has been given the special ability for activating saints into their membership ministry. Christ has given **prophets** His ability to know God's gifts and callings in a person's life. This is not always active in the **prophet**, any more than an evangelist knows which ones are going to be saved when he preaches the gospel. The **prophet's** perception in this area is a higher and more anointed function than the gift of the word of knowledge operating in a saint, just the same as a **prophet** prophesying carries a greater anointing than that of a saint prophesying by the Holy Spirit's gift of prophecy.

The **prophet's** divine enablements are more than gifts of the Holy Spirit. They are the very abilities and graces of Christ Himself. An anointed church member may discern by a word of knowledge that another member has a certain gift or calling, but that does not carry with it the power to perform. It only brings revelation knowledge. When the **prophet** lays hands on and prophesies gifts and callings to a person, his words have the Christ-gifted creative ability to impart, birth, and activate that ministry into the member. If the person receiving the prophetic word does not receive it in faith, it will be a birthing, but it will be stillborn. If the person does not minister to that word of prophecy, it can become malnourished and never reach maturity and life within the individual. There are many other things as well that can hinder a true anointed **prophet's** prophecy from coming to pass in an individual's life and ministry. These hindrances are addressed in another chapter.

The whole Body of Christ will only be built up to full stature and maturity in Christ as every member in the Body is functioning fully in his or her membership ministry. Ephesians

4:16 declares that the Body of Christ is held together by that which every joint supplies, and as each member does its part fully, the body increases and builds itself into a mature, fully functioning body. The **prophet** through his prophesying reveals to members their part to play and helps them to inter-relate properly with other members. Ephesians 4:12 declares that the **prophet** and the other **four** have the primary ministry of equipping the saints with this knowledge and ability so that they can enter into their ministry, thereby causing the whole Body of Christ to be matured.

Christ cannot return until His ascension gift ministries have brought the Church into full manhood. The pastor, evangelist, and teacher have been the only ones acknowledged as being active in this role. But now Christ is activating His **prophets** in the 1980s and His apostles in the 1990s. Jesus is thrilled at the thought that His **prophets** will soon be fully recognized and accepted by His Church. When this happens it will escalate the approach of the consummation of the ages. It will accelerate the "making ready a people for the Lord" so that He can return. It is the prophesying of the **prophets** that brings the Church from a disorganized valley of dry bones to a unified coming together with growth and maturity until the Church arises as an exceeding great and mighty army of the Lord (Ezek. 37:1-14).

CHAPTER 3

THE NATURE OF PROPHECY: SOME DEFINITIONS

In its most broad meaning, prophecy is simply God communicating His thoughts and intents to mankind. When a true prophecy is given, the Holy Spirit inspires someone to communicate God's pure and exact words to the individual or group for whom they are intended. It is delivered without any additions or subtractions by the one prophesying, including any applications or interpretations suggested by the one speaking. To be most effective, it must also be delivered in God's timing and with the proper spirit or attitude.

The prophetic message is usually given vocally. But it may also be written down or acted out symbolically. Prophecy may come to a person as God speaks directly to him, or the Lord may use another person to convey the message.

The Bible as Prophecy

In this sense the whole Bible can rightly be called prophecy—that is, God communicating His thoughts and intents to mankind. The entire Scripture is one inspired revelation of God's mind, will, and word communicated to man and written on paper: *"All Scripture is given by inspiration of God..."* (2 Tim. 3:16). *"For the prophecy came not in old time by the will of man: but holy men of God spake as they were moved by the Holy Ghost"* (2 Pet. 1:21; see also Deut. 6:24; Rev. 1).

The Bible Is God's Complete Revelation to Man. These inspired words were gathered into 66 books and canonized into the Scriptures, the Word of God, the Holy Bible. This prophetic Word is thus complete. It is perfect, fully sufficient to bring all the revelation of God that we can comprehend and appropriate. No further prophetic communication from God is to be added to it and none may be used to subtract from the Bible. Any truly prophetic word given today must therefore be in full agreement with the spirit and context of the Bible.

If this is the case, then, many will ask why we need prophecy at all in the twentieth-century Church. The answer to this question requires first of all that we understand the meaning of two important words from biblical Greek.

Logos—Rhema

Two Greek words in the New Testament are translated by the English term "word": *Logos* and *rhema*. Greek scholars and biblical theologians have debated about whether or not these words are synonymous, but many believe that the inspired writers chose each word to express a different meaning. The interpretation we present here is more consistent with those scholars who are walking in present truth.

When we use the word *Logos*, we refer to the *"Word [Logos] of truth,"* the Scriptures, the Holy Bible (2 Tim. 2:15). St. John also speaks of the "Word" that was in the beginning, that was with God, that was God, and that was made flesh and dwelt among us—none other than our Lord Jesus Christ. Jesus was the eternal Word revealed and manifest in mortal flesh (John 1:1,14).

The *Logos* of God. This *Logos* Word is settled forever in Heaven. Earth and Heaven may pass away, but this Word will never pass away. That part of Scripture which is a description of the Word personage, character, plan, and eternal purpose will never fail, for it is the very expression of God

Himself. The *Logos* is the same as God: the same yesterday, today, and forever.

God's *Logos* is creative, self-fulfilling, powerful, true, inerrant, infallible, complete, and life-giving. It is trustworthy and sure. Any seeming failure or inconsistency in it is due to our failure in understanding, believing, responding, obeying, and seeking to fulfill that unfailing word.

The *Logos*—God's Eternal Standard. The *Logos* is the consistent, absolute standard by which all other expressions, concepts, revelations, doctrines, preachings, and prophecies are measured. The *Logos* reveals God and portrays His eternal principles and decrees. Neither angel, nor human, nor devil, nor any other power in the whole universe can keep the Logos from eternally being and becoming all it proclaims.

***Rhema*—Word.** The *rhema*, on the other hand, might be called "a word from the Word." W.E. Vine's *Expository Dictionary of New Testament Words* explains it this way: "*Rhema* denotes that which is spoken, what is uttered in speech and writing: in the singular, a word. The significance of *rhema* (as distinct from *Logos*) is exemplified in the injunction to take the sword of the Spirit, which is the word (*rhema*) of God" (Eph. 6:17). Here the reference is not to the whole Bible as such, but to the individual scripture which the Spirit brings to our remembrance for use in time of need, a prerequisite being the regular storing of the mind with scripture" (W.E. Vine, *An Expository Dictionary of New Testament Words* [Nashville, Tennessee: Nelson, 1939], p. 1242).

A *rhema*, then, is that timely, Holy Spirit-inspired word from the *Logos* that brings life, power, and faith to perform and fulfill it: *"Faith comes by hearing, and hearing by the word [rhema] of God"* (Rom. 10:17). The *rhema* must be received with faith by the hearer in order for it to fulfill its mission.

***Logos* Prophecy vs. *Rhema* Prophecy.** The *Logos* never changes nor fails, but the Bible is full of *rhemas* given to individuals which failed to come to pass. Actually, however, in these cases it was not the *rhema* of the Lord which failed, but rather the people who heard it failed to understand, interpret, believe, obey, respond, wait upon, or act upon it according to God's will and way. This is the meaning of First Corinthians 13:8: *"Prophecies...shall fail."* When God speaks directly or through a prophet to a person or a nation, and they fail to respond appropriately, the prophecy may not come to pass.

To summarize: When we use the term *Logos*, we mean the Scriptures as a whole. When we use *rhema*, we mean a specific word from the Lord that applies it to us individually. No true *rhema* spoken by a present-day prophet will be in conflict with the spirit and context of the *Logos*.

The *Logos* is like a well of water, and the *rhema* is a bucket of water from that well. The *Logos* is like an entire piano, and the *rhema* is one note sounding forth from it. The *Logos* is like the whole human body, and the *rhema* is one of that body's members performing a particular function. The *rhema* is always dependent on the *Logos*: The body can continue to survive without certain members, but no member can survive without the body.

We all must thank God for the *Logos*, which is the standard of all truth. But we should also be grateful for the *rhema*, which provides the precise word needed for the specific situation. All Christians must live by the *Logos* and receive the *rhema* as needed.

Personal Prophecy Defined. Given this distinction between the *Logos* and the *rhema*, we can now define a **personal prophecy**. When we use this term, we mean God's revelation of His thoughts and intents to a particular person, family, or group of people. It is specific information coming from the mind of God for a specific situation, an inspired word directed to a certain audience.

Personal Prophecy and *Rhema*. In the broad sense, then, personal prophecy is a *rhema*: God's Word individually applied, a word that is subordinate to the *Logos*. This more specific revelation of God's will for our individual lives may come by many ways. A *rhema* may come while reading the

Bible, as God quickens a certain text, or it may come to us through the spoken words of another person.

Personal Prophecy Spoken—*Rhema* Inward Revelation. We will normally use the term **personal prophecy**, however, in a more narrow sense in order to distinguish between divine communications that come straight to us from God and those that come through another human vessel. **Personal prophecy** is what we will call an individual word coming to someone through another human being. *Rhema* is what we will call a word communicated directly by God. This will help us avoid the misunderstanding that we are endorsing the rather dangerous practice of some people who give themselves "personal prophecies."

Personal Work of Holy Spirit But Not Personal Prophecy. The Holy Spirit convicting an individual of sin, and wooing and regenerating that person, is a personal, individual experience, yet it is the same work the Holy Spirit must do to make any sinner into a saint. In a similar way, the illuminating work of the Holy Spirit to bring out the deeper and greater meaning of Scripture is a personal event. But in our use of terms, these situations are rhemas rather than personal prophecy.

General Prophecy in the Bible. Much of the Bible is general prophecy: Scriptures that reveal God's glory, nature, and character; passages that give instructions that are applicable to all mankind; prophetic utterances that deal with general conditions of the world and with the general degeneration of unregenerate man; prophecy about the restoration of the Church and the endtimes; doctrine dealing with sin, repentance, and faith.

***Rhema* Scriptures Give Truth by Illustration.** At the same time, the Bible contains a number of personal prophecies that were given to individuals or groups, and are not universally valid. For example, God's personal prophecy to Noah about building the Ark is not instructions to anyone else (Gen. 6). God's word to Abraham about killing Isaac and offering him as a sacrifice is not directed to present-day Christians (Gen. 22). Jacob's prophetic words concerning each of his son's descendants was specific to them (Gen. 49). And Hosea's prophetic instructions to go marry a harlot (Hosea 1:2) are certainly not for us!

***Rhema*—Personal Prophecy Scriptures Must Not Be Applied Personally Today.** The Bible, in fact, contains countless examples of how God gives personal prophecies to individuals and groups. Even a person with only a little instruction in biblical interpretation knows that these specific instructions are not for everyone. Imagine if a young Christian read in the Bible that God told Isaiah to "walk naked and barefoot in Israel for three years," and then proceeded to do the same in his own city. He might claim, "God told me to do it—it's in the Bible; it's the Word of God!" But no authority, religious or secular, would agree with him. In order to divide rightly the word of truth, then, we must be able to distinguish between the *rhema* of personal prophecy in the Bible and the general word which is the eternal *Logos* for everyone.

UNDERSTANDING "PROPHECY" AND "PERSONAL" PROPHECY
(by Rightly Dividing God's Prophetic Book the Bible, Which Is God's Written *Logos/ Rhema* Word)

"*Logos*" Word	vs.	"*Rhema*" Word
John 1:1,14; 2 Tim. 3:16		Rom. 10:8,17; Eph. 6:17; 2 Cor. 13:1
The "*Logos*" Word		A "*Rhema*" word
The *Word* of God		A word from the *Word*
General prophecies		Personal prophecies
Unconditional prophecies		Conditional prophecies

Thy Word is truth	A true word of God
Truth by declaration	Truth by illustration
Eternal *Word*—God—Jesus	The *Word* speaking specific
Word, same for all eternity	*word* for person, time
Instructions for all people	Instructions for one person
Unchangeable, unfailing	Can fail or be changed
The revelation of God	God revealing and relating
God's prophetic Word	word being prophesied
The wisdom of God	A word of wisdom
The knowledge of God	A word of knowledge
God's thoughts written	One thought personalized
The whole Bible	Individual Scriptures
The throne of God	A thought from the throne

"Logos"	-Illustrations-	*"Rhema"*
The whole human body		One member manifesting
The complete piano		A note sounding forth
The ocean		A wave of ocean water
The sandy seashore		A scoop of that sand
A well of water		Bucket of well water

39 O.T. Books and 27 N.T. Books = 66 Books of THE BIBLE correlated in the third century into one Book called The Holy Scriptures—the inspired written **Word of God—the *Logos*.**

CHAPTER 4

DIVINE HEALING AND PERSONAL PROPHECY

This chapter is placed here to give present-day life experiences in personal prophecy, especially in relation to divine healing. There are seven such chapters (Chps. 4, 6, 8, 10, 12, 15, and 19) that give personal examples of how personal prophecy can minister to every area of life.

Jesus Christ received 39 stripes and suffered indescribable pain to provide healing for our mortal bodies. God supernaturally heals and delivers through several means: the prayer of faith by elders of the church; individuals' direct faith in God; the gifts of healings working through a church member or minister; believing the preaching of the word of faith; and the prophetic word of a prophet that brings deliverance, healing, and creative miracles. This last method is of special interest to us here. What part can personal prophecy play in miraculous healings?

Personal prophecy is not designed to reveal whether God is able or willing to heal. That has been fully substantiated and revealed by the *Logos*, the written Word of God. All present-truth churches have been practicing divine faith healing ever since the Holy Spirit restored this truth back to the Church in the 1880s. ("Present-truth churches" is what I call those who are believing and practicing all truth that has been restored up to the present time.) Much new truth has been restored since the 1880s, and faith healing has increased to include the practice of laying on hands for healing, mass healings, words of knowledge revealing and then healing, gifts of healing, and now healing through a *rhema* or personal prophecy.

It was not till 1979 that I started receiving prophecies from other prophets about healing and miracles taking place in my ministry. Because I had not seen as many miracles in physical healing as I had in the revelation knowledge realm, I assumed that this was not my gift or calling. But after ten to fifteen different prophecies from ministers from different parts of the world concerning God's desire for me to move into the healing realm, I started believing and expecting miraculous healings to take place. Since that time I have seen healings of heart problems, cancer, and numerous other physical problems. I knew the prophetic word was tremendously effective for inner healing, but I had to realize it could be just as effective for bodily healing.

Biblical and pastoral counseling is a vital ministry of the Church for inner healing, and personal prophecy does not replace the need for it. Nevertheless, I have seen God use one flow of a prophetic word to discern the root cause of a problem and speak an anointed word that brings a deliverance to set the person free immediately and permanently.

More can be accomplished by the gifts of the Holy Spirit and the prophet's word and anointing in five minutes than can often be accomplished in numerous hours of normal biblical counseling. Present-truth counselors are now incorporating the gifts of the Holy Spirit and prophetic perception and anointing into their biblical counseling. This makes it truly *biblical* counseling, because it is beyond anything a trained psychiatrist or psychologist can do with only human wisdom and ability.

I have heard many personal prophecies concerning individuals being healed and delivered that were confirmed by miraculous healings and miracles. Yet, sad to say, I have heard more personal prophecies and *rhemas* about people getting healed and being raised from their deathbed that failed to come to pass than those which did. So I am very careful about prophesying that a sick person is going to get well and not die, or that a cripple is going to walk, unless I receive a definite *rhema* word from the Lord.

Probably more prejudice against personal prophecy has come from presumptuous words being given in this area than any other. Why do so many uninspired personal prophecies come forth in this area? How can numerous people give words that a prominent minister who has cancer is going to be healed and live and not die, and yet he dies anyway?

The main cause of this problem is that the person often prophesies from the *Logos* and not from a *rhema*. In other words, they prophesy their doctrine and strong convictions in the Bible, which gives God's general will that divine healing is for all. We can preach, confess, quote, and stand on the *Logos*, but we cannot make it into a personal prophecy to an individual unless the Holy Spirit has quickened it into a *rhema*.

This insight is clarified by comparison to a more basic truth. The Bible declares that Jesus died so that all men may be saved. Technically, everyone was saved when Jesus died on the cross, but that does not mean that everyone is saved or ever will be saved. I cannot go out and prophesy to just anyone, saying, "Thus saith the Lord, you are cleansed from all sin and born again," just because of my strong belief in the vicarious death of Jesus Christ. I can preach to anyone and say, "*If* you will believe on the Lord Jesus Christ, I can assure you that His blood will cleanse you from all sin, and you will be born again."

In the same way, we can preach to a person that God's Word declares that by His stripes we are healed, and Jesus already healed us when He received those 39 stripes, in the same way He saved us when He shed His blood on Calvary. But we cannot *prophesy*, "Thus saith the Lord, you are healed of this disease and you shall not die but live," unless God makes that biblical truth a personal *rhema* for that particular situation. In this sense, there is a big difference between preaching and personal prophecy; between quoting the *Logos* and speaking a *rhema*; between speaking faith statements based on scriptural truth and speaking the specific mind of the Lord for that individual; between speaking *the* Word of God and speaking *a* word from the Lord.

Truth is truth, and the *Logos* and *rhema* are one with God. But Paul declared that faith for specific miracles comes not from our opinions of the *Logos* but rather from a *rhema* from the *Logos*: *"Faith comes by hearing and hearing by the [rhema] of God"* (Rom. 10:17). He declared that the word spoken from our mouth has to come from our heart as a *rhema* in order to be effective: *"The [rhema] is nigh thee, even in thy mouth, and in thy heart: that is, the [rhema] of faith..."* (Rom. 10:8b). The Bible gives the factual knowledge of God, His Word, will, and way, His plan and purpose for mankind. Fact, however, is not faith. But, fact (Scripture) can become faith when it is quickened by the Holy Spirit and mixed with heart belief.

The writer of Hebrews revealed this truth when he said, *"The word [Logos] preached did not profit them, not being mixed with faith in them that heard it"* (Heb. 4:2b). The *Logos* plus the Holy Spirit quickening and faith equals a *rhema* from the Lord. As a *minister* I *preach* the *Logos*, but as a *prophet* I *prophesy* the *rhema*. General biblical truth does not guarantee specific application and appropriation of that truth. A preacher speaks from the letter of the Word which applies to all men for all time, while the prophet speaks from the Spirit of the Word which is personalized to a particular person for a specific situation.

Too often, however, a person speaks from his personal conviction of the scriptural truth of divine healing, yet presents it in the form of a *rhema* or personal prophecy by saying, "God showed me you are going to be healed," or "Thus saith the Lord, I have healed you and you shall live and not die." If the person is not healed from this disease but dies, then that word given is counted as false, even though divine healing is a scriptural truth. This is the main reason so many words given as a personal prophecy or *rhema* fail to come to pass. These doctrinally-directed, instead of divinely inspired, prophecies bring reproach upon the ministry of personal prophecy.

Some of the same problems listed in a later chapter on "Hindrances to Fulfillment of Personal Prophecies" can also hinder people from *giving* a true personal prophecy. The main problems are mind-set, soul blockage, and doctrinal domination that keep us from being Holy Spirit-directed. I would strongly suggest that if you are emotionally involved or have strong personal opinions about a situation, you should abstain from giving a *rhema* or personal prophecy on the matter. Introduce your words instead with "My strong conviction is...I believe that...I am convinced that you will...The Bible declares that..." Do not publicly declare, "Thus says the Lord...God told me...God showed me...The Holy Spirit revealed to me..."

Leave the "Thus saith the Lord" to the mature, proven prophets. They are the ones who are anointed to speak a creative word of healing and miraculous deliverance. Even if a saint or non-prophet minister feels assured that they have a true word from the Lord on the matter, it is still greater wisdom to say, "I am convinced that God is going to..." rather than to say, "God showed me that He will..." It will build the faith of others just as much, and if it works as you confessed it would, then you will get credit that your convictions were right. If it does not happen as you believed and confessed it would, then you will not be subject to being called a false prophet or prophesier. Rather you will simply have spoken what you believed to be the truth on the matter.

No one who believes in divine healing will blast you for believing and confessing your convictions on divine healing, even when you direct it to a specific person's healing. But if you put your convictions in the form of *rhema* or personal prophecy and it does not come to pass, then you may justly be judged and proclaimed a false representative of the mind of God in the matter. Your presumptuous prophesying will also bring reproach on the gift of prophecy, the ministry of prophesying, and the office of the prophet.

Probably 99 percent of all the healing and miracles I personally know about that happened through personal prophecy occurred when the one prophesying had no prior knowledge of the existing condition. Numerous prophets could give hundreds of testimonies of healing and miracles that have happened in their ministry, and I think all of them would agree with this percentage. Once there is natural knowledge and personal involvement in a situation, it is much, much harder to receive a pure and clear word on the matter. It is much easier to speak a creative word of healing from a Holy Spirit-inspired rhema than from our own beliefs concerning the doctrine of the *Logos*. I have seen both take place, but by far the majority have come when I speak an inspired rhema in personal prophecy and prophetic praying.

Present-day Examples. A few testimonies will show how this can work. The first comes from a pastor and his wife who pastored a growing church in the late '70s. This couple had established a CI extension college in their church, so I ministered there a couple of times a year. I had prophesied over the pastor and his wife each time I was there during those years.

Of the numerous examples that could be given, this story best portrays the problems with personal prophecies in relation to divine healing.

The doctors discovered that the wife had cancer cells in her blood stream, but could not determine their origination without exploratory surgery. We laid hands on her, and God showed me the place in her body where the problem originated. It was in a different spot from where the physicians expected it to be.

She told the surgeons that another doctor (she didn't explain it was a "Doctor of Prophetic Insight") had diagnosed her problem as located in this particular area, and asked them to check that area during exploratory surgery. They could not find a problem where they expected it to be, so they looked where the other doctor had suggested. The source of the cancer cells was discovered. The pastor called and requested prophetic insight as to whether his wife should take the chemotherapy treatments as the doctors requested. God spoke this prophetic word for him to give to her:

"If she takes the chemotherapy treatments she will feel better and the cancer will go into remission for two years, but then it will come back worse than ever. If she will trust God wholly for divine healing, she will suffer for a while and have to battle through in faith, but will be completely healed within two years."

I do not know how clearly he conveyed that word to his wife, no more than I know how clearly Adam conveyed God's instructions to his wife concerning God's word about the tree of the knowledge of good and evil. But the next time I heard from them, she was taking the treatments and gaining some relief. The cancer was going into remission.

Two years later I was in a Sunday night service in their church. The pastor's wife was home in bed because the cancer had reactivated and spread so fast that her condition was inoperable. After prayer for her in church, the associate pastor, who had a prophetic call upon his life, stood to his feet and prophesied emphatically and specifically that God would heal her and raise her off that deathbed for His glory, and that it would be a great witness to the surrounding community. A few others were inspired by his prophecy to prophesy words of power and victory and healing, but they did not name her in their prophecies as he did.

My prophetic spirit did not witness that they were prophesying from a *rhema* or the mind of the Lord on this matter. I felt they were prophesying from their doctrine of the *Logos*, love for the pastor's wife, and their zeal to see a miracle manifested. The next morning on the way to the airport we went to her bedside to minister to her. My wife and I prayed and I prophesied to her. There was nothing in the prophetic word about a miraculous healing, though I was personally believing for a prophetic word of miraculous healing and life. There were many words of comfort, and God's assurance concerning her children and husband. She had been in great pain and had become very cantankerous and uncooperative. But after the prophecy, great peace came to her, the joy of the Lord returned, her attitude changed, and the smile she used to have all the time returned.

We were told later that after we left, she began to make restitution with certain people and family members. She arranged the songs and service to have at her home-going. I flew back a few weeks later to preach her funeral, and participated in her home-going service. While there I counseled the young associate pastor who had given the specific prophecy about her healing. He was devastated in his life, reputation, and ability to prophesy the true word of the Lord. But after much counsel and prayer he was able to adjust, renew, and press on.

The counseling included thoughts on proper prophetic motivation, hindrances to giving true prophecies, and the need of prophets being trained and under apprenticeship to an older mature prophet—as Elisha was to Elijah—before giving such serious specific words. I reassured him that he was not a false prophet, but rather his immaturity, zeal, and biblical convictions had motivated him to give a presumptuous prophecy. He was to let it be a humbling, learning process to prepare him to be a mature prophet.

This presumptuous prophecy was just one of the many problems that caused the church to go from four hundred to forty people during the next few years. One of the problems was that the pastor became disillusioned and resentful to God over the death of his wife. He began to take his frustrations out on the people by preaching hard at them instead of ministering to them. I had given him a prophetic word that he should preach for the next six months on the healing virtue of Christ, Christ's victory over all things, and miraculous power. He ignored that word and preached negative thoughts, criticized the people, and took his frustrations out in his preaching. He finally left the church after it had dwindled to 40. His son-in-law took it over, and has worked for years to restore the people gradually and to reestablish the work.

Just as true prophecies will bring blessings, prosperity, and miracles, so will immature, presumptuous, and false prophecies bring destruction, confusion, and failure. The answer is not to reject or despise prophets, personal prophecy, and congregational prophesying, but rather to teach, train, and mature the saints and young prophets in the prophetic realm.

One interesting sidelight from this situation came from the dying woman's comments to me. She said:

"Dr. Bill, I have read over all the pages of prophecies that you have given to me over the years, and everything you said I would do has come to pass. I have done and become all that the prophecies said that I would do and be."

I use her situation to encourage people who have portions of their personal prophecies that have not come to pass yet, saying, "Don't become discouraged because all your prophecies have not been fulfilled. Be encouraged, for the only person who ever told me all her prophecies had been fulfilled died within three weeks." If God keeps talking about things you are going to do in years to come, it means that if you are obedient, then you have many years yet to live and do the will of God.

Evangelists who have power gifts can be told what the physical condition is, and they can pray and minister with the gift of healing and word of faith to perform miracles. But they rarely prophesy ahead of time that the person is going to be healed. Most miracles take place through personal prophecy during the time the prophetic word is flowing to the individual. A couple of present-day testimonies will amplify this truth.

A New Heart. One young Christian man at the age of 29 was successfully operating four businesses. He had forced himself to work 16 to 20 hours a day for years, to come to this place of success. Though a Christian, he still had continually broken

God's laws of rest and temperance, and was now suffering the consequences in his body.

After intensive examinations and tests in the hospital, it was determined that he had a serious heart condition and blood circulation problems. So he had to take strong medications which made him unable to work. The doctor's prognosis was that he would have to be on medication the rest of his life, and have open heart surgery. Five years later, things were no better and his life expectancy was about six months. Let him give you the rest of his testimony in his own words:

I continued on until April 8, 1984. At that time, Dr. Hamon, you were conducting a Holy Spirit seminar at our church. That night you preached, and at the close of the message you asked all the leadership in the church to come forward and line up across the front. My wife and I went up. (Keep in mind that we had never seen or heard of you before this.)

You laid hands on us and started to prophesy. You prophesied many things that I had gone through, and many things about what God was going to do in my life and ministry. Right in the middle of the flow of your prophesying, without asking me if I had any physical problems, you began to speak, "Heal him, Lord, heal him, Lord, give him a new heart, give him a new circulatory system."

I fell to the floor, and the power of God began to surge throughout my body. I instantly knew that God had restored my health. For over an hour afterwards I could feel the blood circulating in the ends of my fingers and toes. It felt like something was washing out my entire circulatory system.

A few months later I had a physical, and the doctors verified that there were no signs of my ever having had a heart or circulatory problem. So I poured the medicine out and filled the bottles with olive oil to anoint people for prayer and to testify about my healing.

One year later I had an opportunity to give my testimony at one of your prophet seminars. That was on Thursday night, and the next night I was playing softball with the church team. Suddenly, I began to experience extreme pain in my chest and down my left arm. I began to double over with pain. I thought I would have to be carried off the field, but in a few minutes the pain left as suddenly as it had come.

The following Sunday, I was telling my pastor about what had happened and he informed me that he was at the CI seminar on that Friday night. He stated that you had suddenly stopped right in the middle of the service and revealed that God was showing you that the devil was trying right then to put the heart condition back on the man who had given his testimony the night before about being healed. You had the people to stand and point in the general direction of Panama City where I lived. You took authority over the enemy and commanded him to leave permanently. We determined that that was exactly the same time I was having the symptoms of a heart attack on the ball field.

From that time in 1984 till now, in 1987, I have had no further symptoms or problems. In fact, I have been issued a life insurance policy as a preferred risk. I praise God that there are prophets in the Church today. The word you gave about me going into spiritual ministry has also come to pass. I have now been ordained and am in spiritual ministry for my Lord and Savior Jesus Christ.

A Vision. In October, 1981, the Lord gave me one of the few visions I have seen in my lifetime. While worshiping at a CI seminar with eyes closed and hands uplifted to God, I suddenly saw in blazing letters written across my forehead, "Power over cancer and heart problems." Before I mentioned it to anyone else, a brother came to me and said, "While you were worshiping the Lord, I looked at you and saw written across your forehead in large red letters, 'Power over cancer and heart problems.' " So I accepted it as a true vision, but explained to God that I did not know why He was giving that to me when I could not even find enough time to fulfill my prophet and personal prophecy ministry.

I did not mention this publicly until one night in Pensacola, Florida, when the Holy Spirit prompted me to do so. There was a lady there who had had a battle with recurring cancer for years. As soon as she received a miracle of healing in one area of her body, the cancer would recur in another part of her body. Here is the part of the testimony that deals with her final and complete victory:

Finally, I had cancer in my throat. In desperation, I called out to God and told Him I had done and was doing all I knew to do. I really needed help, or I would lose this long fight against cancer.

It was on November 18, 1981, when I called out to God for some answer about why I could not keep my healing. The Holy Spirit impressed me to go to a church on Jackson Street called Amazing Grace. I had no transportation of my own, but God provided a way for me to go.

I had already heard Dr. Bill twice at our church, Liberty Fellowship, in June of 1981. I just knew in my spirit that this was my night for a miracle healing that would last, but I was not prepared for what happened. Dr. Bill said that God had made known that He had given him power over cancer, and if anyone had been diagnosed as having cancer cells in their body to come down for prayer. I was the only one that came forward.

Dr. Bill prayed in the Spirit for awhile and then started speaking loud and authoritatively, "Father, we smite this cancer now, and curse the very root cause in the name of Jesus. I tear you loose from the root, come out, set her free, loose her, come out now and go from her forever."

That foul spirit that had been reactivating cancer in my body for the last seven years screamed out of me and tore at my body, but you spoke out again for him to harass me no longer, but be gone from me forever. Thank God he left, I was healed completely, and I am still healed after all these years—and will continue to be.

I thank God that our Lord Jesus has given men power in His name to deliver His people from the destructive forces of the enemy. Thank you for being obedient and speaking out that night. I am finally completely set free of recurring cancer. Praise God!

I have prayed for many people with cancer and heart problems. Very few are healed when the request is made and we simply respond in obedience to the commands of the *Logos*. But almost everyone is healed when the need is made known by revelation knowledge and prophetic praying.

Because Jesus healed everyone who came to Him, those who minister divine healing become frustrated that they do not see everyone healed. But Jesus was the only one who had fullness of the Spirit, faith, and power. We minister according to our divinely gifted abilities, which come far short of sufficient faith to heal all with whom we come in contact. Nevertheless, we will continue to exercise all the faith and anointing for healing and miracles we have, continually believing for greater miracles and a higher percentage of positive results. This much we do know and have proven over and over again: Personal prophecy and prophetic praying, when divinely directed, bring miraculous results within those who receive the ministry.

CHAPTER 5

FIVE CHANNELS OF PROPHECY

In addition to Scripture (and always subordinate to it), God's prophetic word to His people usually comes through one of five channels. To understand how God communicates to us prophetically, we must know the differences between them. These are the five:

The Office of Prophet (Eph. 2:20; 4:11; 1 Cor. 12:28; Acts 13:1)

The ministry of the prophet in the Church is not a gift of the Holy Spirit, but a gift-extension of Christ Himself as the Prophet. Jesus Christ was the full manifestation of the offices of Apostle, Prophet, Evangelist, Pastor, and Teacher all in one human body. After His ascension into Heaven, the fivefold ministry He had embodied on earth was sent back as gifts to the Church in the form of men who filled those offices. No one person received all five, but some received one (Eph. 4:11).

This gifting was not an external endowment like a birthday present. Instead, it was an investment of Christ's mantle for one of the five ministries of Jesus—a divine impartation of Christ's own nature, wisdom, and power for each particular kind of performance. All five, when moving in full maturity, represent Christ's full ministry to the Church.

These ministries are not just an extension of Body ministry, but an extension of the headship of Christ to His Body, the Church.

The one gifted as an apostle received that portion of Christ's mantle that enabled Jesus to be the great Apostle of the faith. The evangelist received Christ's evangelistic anointing. The pastor was given Christ's Good Shepherd heart and staff, and the teacher, Christ's divine teaching ability. Finally, the prophet received those attributes of Christ that endowed Him with the ability to perceive what was in the heart of people, to proclaim the future counsels and purposes of God, and to know the secret things of God.

The office of the prophet is designed and endowed to function in a higher realm of ministry than the Holy Spirit's gift of prophecy. This gift of prophecy operates within the saints or a minister for the general upbuilding, encouraging, and comforting of the Church (1 Cor. 12:10; 14:3-4). But the office of prophet is authorized and anointed to do much more.

The prophet, in fact, has administrative authority. The prophet has the same authority to minister to the church with his preaching and prophesying as the pastor does with his preaching and pastoral counseling. Church prophets function in all the ministries of the Old Testament prophets, as well as the New Testament gift of the prophet standing in the role of Christ, the Prophet. Thus their prophecies flow in the areas of guidance, instruction, rebuke, judgment, and revelation—whatever Christ chooses to speak for the purifying and perfecting of His Church.

Prophets, then, are more than pastors speaking with the gift of prophecy. In the New Testament Church structure they are secondary only to the apostles: *"God hath set some in the church, first apostles, secondarily prophets..."* (1 Cor. 12:28). Paul tells us that the ministries of apostles and prophets are foundational to the building of Christ's Church (Eph. 2:20-22). They are a direct extension of the "Cornerstone," Jesus, to give alignment and proper structure to God's building, the Church. So any local church that is established without an apostle or prophet ministry will not have a proper foundation for maximum growth.

Prophets have been active in the Church during its nearly 20 centuries of existence, but after the Church fell into apostasy they ceased to be recognized as such, especially by the generation to whom they ministered. But I believe the time has come when Christ Jesus is determined to bring recognition to His prophets. All fivefold ministries must be restored to the Church before it can be ready for Christ's return (Acts 3:21).

The prophets are especially anointed to perceive what is next on God's agenda for restoration. Then they lift their voices like trumpets to alert, enlighten, and charge the Church to conquer that part of the truth to be restored at that time. The prophets are the eyes of the Body of Christ, the trumpeters in the army of the Lord to give a clear sound revealing the desires of the Commander in Chief.

I believe that the decade of the 1980s has been designated in the counsels of God as the time for the calling forth of the prophet ministry. Before the 1980s are over, God will have raised up and called forth thousands of prophets. Their ministry will be clarified and amplified until all the present-truth church world recognizes them as ordained by God and gifts of God to the Church. They will no longer be denied and ignored, but rather accepted and activated into their full, anointed authority within the office of prophet. For the Holy Spirit has been commissioned by Christ, the Head of the Church, to bring forth and prepare the prophets for their day of presentation and performance.

Christ declared that Elijah, the prophet, must first come before He Himself could be fully manifest in His role as Messiah. John the Baptist fulfilled that prophecy for Christ's first coming. The emerging company of prophets with the prophetic mantle of Elijah will prepare the way for Christ's second coming in full manifestation of His ministry as King of kings and Lord of lords. The cry of the Holy Spirit is for prophets to come forth. The Church is crying out for holy and truly

God-anointed prophets. And the prophets are coming, for the Spirit and the Bride are now saying, "Come!"

Prophetic Preaching (1 Pet. 4:11)

Preaching and prophesying are not the same thing. Preaching is normally speaking biblical truths that have been researched, studied, and arranged for presentation. Prophecy is normally extemporaneous, by divine inspiration and revelation knowledge. Preaching proclaims the *Logos*, while prophecy gives a rhema from the *Logos*. Both are the Word of God.

Prophetic preaching is not the same as simply getting the mind of the Lord about which sermon to preach on Sunday, or being anointed to preach a specially prepared message from the Bible. It is a different realm altogether. Any one of the fivefold ministries (apostle, prophet, evangelist, pastor, teacher—Eph. 4:11) may at times enter into prophetic ministry as he preaches.

Such prophetic preaching from biblical truths is the direct voice of God with the pure mind of Christ, so that even the speaker's precise words and illustrations are exactly what God wants to say to the people present in that place at that time. Though the minister does not preface his statements with "Thus saith the Lord," the words are just as inspired and anointed as if a prophet were to speak using that phrase. Prophetic preaching is the "oracle of God" (1 Pet. 4:11).

The Prophetic Presbytery (1 Tim. 4:14; Heb. 6:1-2; Acts 13:1-3)

A third channel for prophetic ministry is the laying on of hands with prophecy by men and women of God who meet the qualifications of presbyter. The presbytery serves several functions in this regard, each one calling for a different set of qualifications both in the presbyters and in the candidates:

1. ***Prophetic revelation and confirmation*** of those called to leadership ministry in the Church.

2. ***Ordination to the fivefold ministry.*** This is the laying on of hands for authorization and recognition as an ordained minister of God.

3. ***Confirmation and activation*** of membership ministries in the Body of Christ.

4. ***Progress*** in Christian maturity.

We will trace these functions in detail in another volume of this series, but for now we should note that the laying on of hands is the fourth of the six doctrines of Christ that a person must experience to go on to maturity (Heb. 6:1-2). Every Christian needs the blessing and benefits of laying on of hands and prophecy by God-anointed and leadership-appointed ministry in the Church.

We should also note that the prophetic presbytery does not eliminate the need for the individual office of prophet. All ministers and others in church leadership can exercise their faith and speak a word of prophecy over an individual while functioning as a presbytery team member. But only a prophet can minister in that prophetic realm ordained for the office of the prophet.

The prophet's ministry is, in fact, ordained to function in all the realms of the prophetic presbytery, as well as to fulfill the office of prophet. Prophets are anointed to do on an individual basis all that the prophetic presbytery does as a team.

One difference, however, is that the prophetic presbytery is given the honor of extending formal and final ordination to a ministry. The prophet may reveal a person's call to fivefold ministry, and lay hands upon him to anoint him for it. But ordination is performed by the presbytery.

In the Old Testament there were two groups that recognized and anointed men for leadership ministry. The first, the Aaronic priesthood, laid on hands for ordaining Levites and priests. Both the priests and their candidates had to meet a number of stipulations and requirements in this process.

The other group to recognize and anoint leadership was the prophets. They did not have the same system of restrictions as the priests; the prophets simply spoke to the one God pointed out. They called out and anointed whomever God indicated without regard to any other factor. An example of such a choice is provided in Samuel's anointing of David for kingship—a youth in his early teens.

These two Old Testament groups have their counterparts in the Church. The prophetic presbytery is parallel to the Aaronic priesthood. Like that ancient priesthood, many church leaders have established numerous requirements for leadership. These stipulations are not necessarily found in Scripture, but they are sound guidelines developed over the years.

The modern-day prophets are parallel to those of the Old Testament. They, too, function without the restrictions of the "priesthood" presbytery. Today's prophetic presbytery would not even consider a young man like David for candidacy for prophetic presbytery, but a church prophet might nevertheless call him out of the congregation, lay hands on him, prophesy his calling, and anoint him for that ministry. The prophetic presbytery (after the Aaronic priesthood order which was restored in 1948) would not allow themselves to prophesy to a 13-year-old that he is called to be an apostle (king). But the prophet is free to follow the leading of the Lord without the limitations and restrictions of the prophetic presbytery.

Every minister needs to be anointed properly with formal ordination to their ascension gift ministry. Every saint needs a prophetic presbytery for membership ministry, confirmation, and activation. The prophetic presbytery is a vital ministry in the New Testament Church.

The Gift of Prophecy (Acts 2:17; 1 Cor. 12:10; 14:1,3-4,6,22,24,31,39; 1 Thess. 5:20; Rom. 12:6)

Prophecy is one of the nine manifestations of the Holy Spirit listed in First Corinthians 12. Verse 7 declares that the manifestation is given; it is a gift, a grace, an unmerited divine enablement. It is not given on the basis of Christian maturity, but because Christ wants to bless His Church through this gift and the others. So these gifts are received and administered by grace and faith.

The Holy Spirit has all nine gifts, but He distributes them to individual saints as He wills. He has willed that every born-again, Spirit-filled saint be endowed with one or more of them. These gifts are not given for self-edification, but for the edification of the whole Body of Christ.

The one exception to this rule is the gift of unknown tongues. According to the apostle Paul, the main purpose for this gift is to build up the inner man for self-edification: *"He that speaketh in an unknown tongue edifieth himself; but he that prophesieth edifieth the church....He that speaketh in an unknown tongue speaketh not unto men, but unto God....But he that prophesieth speaketh unto men to edification, and exhortation, and comfort"* (1 Cor. 14:4,2-3).

Tongues spoken out in a public meeting are not profitable to the church congregation unless they are interpreted in the language of the people present. But tongues with interpretation have the same benefits as prophecy: *"For greater is he that prophesieth than he that speaketh with tongues, except he interpret, that the church may receive edifying"* (1 Cor. 14:5b). This edification of the Church should in fact be the primary motivation of the saints in desiring to minister spiritual gifts: *"Forasmuch as ye are zealous of spiritual gifts, seek that ye may excel to the edifying of the church....Let all things be done unto edifying"* (1 Cor. 14:12,26b).

For this reason, prophecy is important in the life of the Church, because prophecy is the most edifying gift for a congregation. The other eight are focused "rifle" gifts, which normally bless one specific person or perhaps a few; prophecy is a "shotgun" gift that can bless hundreds of people at once.

This is one reason why Paul told the saints at Corinth to *"desire spiritual gifts, but rather that ye may* **prophesy**.... *Wherefore, brethren,* **covet** *to* **prophesy**" (1 Cor. 14:1,39a, emphasis added). He told the Thessalonians to *"despise not prophesyings"* (1 Thess. 5:20). And to the church at Rome he wrote: *"Having then gifts differing according to the grace that is given to us, whether prophecy, let us prophesy according to the proportion of faith"* (Rom. 12:6). Prophesying was evidently a common event in all the churches Paul established. Paul said he proclaimed the Word of God by four different means: *"I shall speak to you either by revelation, or by knowledge, or by prophesying, or by doctrine"* (1 Cor. 14:6b).

Peter taught the same truths about spiritual manifestations among the saints: *"As every man hath received the gift, even so minister the same one to another, as good stewards of the manifold grace of God"* (1 Pet. 4:10). A New Testament church that is functioning on the same foundation that was laid by the first apostles and prophets will have manifestations of the Holy Spirit, especially the prophetic gift, in all its activities.

We must keep in mind that the gift of prophecy is not the same as the office of prophet. Rather, it is an extension of the ministry of the Holy Spirit, while the office of prophet is an extension of the ministry of Christ. The gift is a body ministry function, while the office is a headship function.

The Spirit of Prophecy and Prophetic Song

The spirit of prophecy is the testimony of Jesus (Rev. 19:10). This is not a gift or office, but an anointing arising from Christ within the believer. It takes place on occasions of special anointing in a service, or when Christians exercise their faith to be a voice through which Christ can testify.

Those who are not prophets or do not have the gift of prophecy will normally not prophesy; but when the spirit of prophecy is present, they may do so. This often happens under one of three conditions:

A **mighty prophetic presence** of the Lord permeates the service, making it easier to prophesy than to keep silent.

People come among a **company of prophets** or under the mantle of an anointed prophet.

People are **challenged by a minister** to let God arise and testify through them by the spirit of prophecy.

At these times any saint can enter in and exercise faith to prophesy: *"Let us prophesy according to the proportion of faith"* (Rom. 12:6b). *"For ye may all prophesy one by one, that all may learn, and all may be comforted"* (1 Cor. 14:31). Those who prophesy under these circumstances should not assume that they have a gift of prophecy or office of a prophet. But if they keep exercising their faith in this way, a confirmation by a prophet or prophetic presbytery may make known to what extent they are called to the prophetic realm.

In Numbers 11:24-30, the 70 elders of Israel all prophesied when God took of the prophetic spirit on Moses and placed it upon them. At that time two men began to prophesy apart from the others, and Joshua told Moses to stop them. But Moses replied with his famous declaration: *"Would God that all the Lord's people were prophets* [prophesiers], *and the Lord would put His Spirit upon them!"* Again, in First Samuel 10:10, Saul met a company of prophets, and the spirit of prophecy came upon him so that he began to prophesy. These stories should encourage those who want to learn to prophesy that they should find a prophet or company of prophets to train them how to release their faith so they can move in the spirit of prophecy.

The **song of the Lord** (Col. 3:16) is the spirit of prophecy expressing the thoughts and desires of Christ in song. The Scripture says of Jesus that *"in the midst of the church"* He would *"sing praises to God"* (Heb. 2:12) and that God *"will joy over thee with singing"* (Zeph. 3:17b). Prophetic song is part of the nature of Christ. He is a singing Savior, and He wants to sing to His Church by the spirit of prophecy. Any saint may participate in this, but the anointing is mightier when the song comes through a prophet, prophetess, or one with a gift of prophecy.

Understandably, a person with a melodious voice is best used in this fashion. I myself receive many good words from the Lord, and some of them are even in rhyme; but since I do not have a good singing voice for the Holy Spirit to use, I refrain from singing the prophetic song. For me to sing a prophecy that would bless the ears as well as the spirit, God would not only have to give a prophetic anointing; He would also have to work a miracle in my voice. So I sing prophetically to the Lord when I am alone with Him, but I prophesy unsung words when with other people.

Throughout the Bible we read again and again that we are to *"sing unto the Lord a new song"* (Ps. 33:3; 40:3; 96:1; 98:1; 144:9; 149:1; Isa. 42:10). Even the Book of Revelation reveals that when all the redeemed of the ages are gathered together, they will sing a new song (Rev. 5:9; 14:3). Prophetic singing is a part of the restoration of the prophetic realm. Singing is an activity of God and of the eternal Church. I believe that "spiritual songs" are the same as prophetic songs, so we should continue *"teaching and admonishing one another in Psalms and hymns and spiritual songs"* (Col. 3:16b).

CHAPTER 6

PERSONAL PROPHECIES CONCERNING MINISTRIES, GIFTS, AND CALLINGS

Each member in the Body of Christ has a special membership ministry to fulfill. The Holy Spirit distributes gifts and talents to every child of God, and Jesus calls some to be apostles, prophets, evangelists, pastors, or teachers. Personal prophecy can play an important role in helping saints come to know their place and function in the Church.

How do Christians come to know their particular calling, gift, or ministry anointing? Biblical examples reveal numerous ways: dreams, visions, supernatural manifestations, the voice of God, an angelic visitation, or the Holy Spirit's witness and illumination of a Scripture that becomes a *rhema* to the individual. With some, God simply placed a strong desire within to be a minister of the Gospel. In the case of the 12 apostles, Jesus issued a call by personal invitation. After His resurrection, the Lord appeared to Paul in His resurrected human body in brilliant light and called the apostle personally. Then He sent to him a disciple with a prophetic anointing who could lay hands upon him and prophesy more details concerning his ministry as an apostle of the Church to the Gentiles. In the

Old Testament, David came to know his kingship ministry by personal prophecy from the prophet Samuel. In the New Testament, Timothy came to know his gifts and calling by the laying on of hands and prophecy by Paul and the prophetic presbytery.

Evidently, God has never limited Himself to one method of calling. If you are a minister, think back to how you were initially called, how the call was confirmed, and how God worked it out for you to be in your present ministry. Probably no two calls are exactly alike. If you are not an ordained minister, how were you called to your ministry as a member of the Body of Christ? If you do not yet know your membership ministry, you need to discover it, just as much as a minister needs to know which of the fivefold ascension gifts he has received.

Thank God for the restoration of the prophet and personal prophecy. Ministries can now be made known to those who do not know their ministry, and confirmed to those who do. Since every member must come to full membership ministry before the Church can reach maturity and be properly prepared for the coming of the Lord, we can understand why Christ is restoring His prophet ministry to the Church as He ordained it should be.

My Own Calling to Ministry

My call to the ministry did not involve a vision, dream, angelic visitation, or voice from Heaven. Though most people think that in order to be a prophet you must have some unusual supernatural experience, I received nothing of that nature. All I received was a growing desire after I was saved to become a minister.

I prayed by the hour and fasted up to seven days at a time for some supernatural manifestation and heavenly confirmation of this desire for ministry. I sought such a confirmation because I had no way of knowing whether it was my own ambition or Jesus calling and the Holy Spirit prompting. God's providential happenings eventually brought me into ministry, but it was two years after I became a pastor before I received any confirmation outside of my own desire and conviction that I was called into full-time, fivefold ministry.

The prophecies that came over me in 1953 by the ministerial presbytery described the activities, gifts, and ministry of someone who would be a minister, but not once did they mention any fivefold ministerial office nor use the word *preacher* or *minister*. So during the first two years of my pastoral ministry I questioned whether or not I was really called. But great assurance and encouragement came when in 1956 a prophet called me out of the audience and gave a half-page prophecy with the closing statement: "Lo, I have called thee as a prophet of these last days. Though it seemeth slow to be, yet I shall perfect that which concerneth thee." Finally, I had a clear confirmation that I was called, and specifically to the office of the prophet.

I have concluded since then that one reason God did not give me the visions, dreams, and supernatural visitations I begged, pleaded, fasted, and prayed for by the hour was that He was preparing me for the time when I would become one of His instruments to pioneer and propagate the restoration ministry of prophets and personal prophecy. He wanted me to have an appreciation for this ministry. If I had been able to find out everything about my ministry on my own without other ministers and saints being used to prophesy new ministries and callings, I would not have been willing in later years to stand for hours and prophesy over hundreds of others. I probably would have thought instead, "*I* prayed and sought God and found out *my* calling by myself. God told *me*, and if others want to know, they will just have to pay the price I did so God will speak to them as He did to me."

Through God's calling, preparation, and anointing, He has enabled me to prophesy to over 15,000 people. During these 35 years of prophetic ministry, I have prophesied to hundreds of ministers and brought revelation and confirmation to their ascension gift calling. God has often led me to call out men in the audience who were not in the ministry, and reveal to them that they have a call to a special ministry. To some the thought of being a minister had never crossed their mind—it was a brand new revelation to them.

One such testimony concerns a prophecy on the very same night God first opened the endless river of prophetic flow through me. I prophesied over a businessman who was president of the local Full Gospel Business Men's Fellowship. His children were grown and he was well established in business with no thought of becoming a minister or missionary. This is his report:

My wife and I were at a meeting in Sacramento, California, in January, 1973. I was sitting on the platform and my wife was sitting in the audience. Dr. Hamon was prophesying to different individuals under a strong anointing. He pointed to my wife in the audience and then to me on the platform, and asked if we belonged to each other. We said yes, and he called us to him and gave us a prophecy.

The prophecy included statements declaring that God had called us to the ministry and that within one year we would be in another country preaching the Gospel. I did not relate to that, nor did I believe it could be God. But 11 months later God called us to be missionaries in Mexico. At the writing of this testimony we have now been ministering in Mexico for eight years.

Another testimony comes from a man who has been a youth pastor for several years. This second report also shows that prophets will often speak things concerning ministry that had never before been considered by the person receiving the prophecy:

Dr. Hamon, you prophesied to me that I would raise up the children's church and the youth ministry, for God had anointed me for that ministry. You prophesied that they are the Church of today and the leadership of tomorrow, and I was to minister to this part of His Church and prepare His leadership.

When I walked outside the church, I was in shock. I had not been around prophets much, and because I had never thought of that ministry or had a desire to minister to children and youth, I began to think you had missed it. The immediate ministry you prophesied to me was completely opposite to what I thought God wanted me to do in the ministry. I even thought that maybe my pastor had paid you off to prophesy that word over me!

I had never worked with children before. I had my own ideas of what I could do and should do in the ministry, and it did not include children's ministry. But that prophecy completely changed my direction, my thinking, and my life! Because of my previous mind-set concerning my ministry, I did not immediately relate to what you said. Yet I acted in faith upon 2 Chronicles 20:20 and believed His prophets so I would prosper. My pastor was in full agreement with the word, so he appointed us to the youth ministry. God has prospered the ministries to children and youth mightily.

This brother and his wife have done an outstanding job with the children's church and youth ministry. During the last four years they have produced one of the most successful youth ministries in any church. They love it now, and find great fulfillment in their ministry as youth pastors.

Activating Ministry by Personal Prophecy. Personal prophecy that is truly directed by the Holy Spirit is God speaking. When God speaks something, it is decreed in Heaven. It is impregnated into the spirit of the person receiving the word of the Lord, and God's word carries with it the creative, life-giving power of self-fulfillment.

The reception of the divine, prophetic word is like conception in the womb of a woman or the planting of hybrid corn seed within the ground. The baby will grow and be born if the woman does nothing to abort the process. The seed will germinate and grow to a full stalk of corn with one or two large ears if the farmer waters, cultivates, weeds, and sprays against disease and worms.

Personal prophecy from the prophets and prophetic presbytery is one of God's ordained methods for planting the seed of ministry and gifts within individuals. The anointing that flows with the prophetic word is like the yeast that makes bread rise or the water that makes seeds in dry ground sprout. Ministry can be activated by personal prophecy and the prophetic anointing, but it takes discipline, diligence, and continual development to bring that ministry to consistency and maturity with mightier manifestations. Of the fivefold ascension gift ministers, the prophets have the strongest anointing and ministry for impartation and activation of gifts and ministries.

We must keep in mind that this ministry will not work through self-appointed prophesiers trying to speak as prophets. It will not work through someone speaking presumptuous, prophetic faith statements to fulfill their own ideas and desires. The thoughts spoken must have originated in the mind and will of God to be creatively productive.

There are always those who learn of a truth and then try to produce it through faith formulas, theological teaching, and doctrinal disciplines. But this is a work of the Spirit through a God-ordained prophet ministry. Any substitute is a counterfeit. It will be nonproductive and more of a hindrance than a help to the person giving and the individual receiving the non-anointed word.

When personal prophecy is flowing in divine order, however, it will impregnate and activate ministry within church members and ministers. Here are two examples from among many of those who have had this principle proven in their lives.

A pastor from North Carolina attended one of our CI Holy Spirit/prophet seminars in 1985. He sat under the teaching on how to activate the gifts of the Holy Spirit within our life, and was ministered to, both by me and the prophetic presbytery which is formed from CI's staff and the company of prophets present. (Normally, there are three prophets per prophetic team, and one or two standing with the team for training and activation.) This pastor received several prophecies concerning many areas of his life. The Lord had me prophesy specific gifts and ministries that were going to be manifested in his life, including the word of knowledge and prophetic anointing for calling people out and ministering to them personal prophecy and divine healing.

We were talking afterward and he explained to me that he appreciated the words and the enthusiasm of those who ministered, but he just did not minister in those areas. He said that he had traveled with one of the outstanding healing ministers who manifests the gifts of the Spirit, but it just never worked in him. He did not doubt that God could some day use him that way, but it did not relate to him now.

Nevertheless, that pastor called us back the following week with this glowing report. When he arrived back home and began to minister on Sunday morning, the Holy Spirit began to stir him and his faith was activated—and he began to do exactly as the personal prophecy said he would do. By 1:30 that afternoon he was still calling people out by a word of knowledge and prophesying to them and ministering healing to those needs that God made known supernaturally. The prophetic word had impregnated and activated the gifts and anointing for that ministry.

In addition, God used a little situation to make sure the pastor exercised his faith and allowed God to do this for him. He had brought one of his new converts to the seminar with him. On the way home the young Christian said to him, "Isn't it exciting, Pastor, what God is going to do through you Sunday when we get back home? You remember what God said through the prophets you were going to do when you got back home?" He either had to discredit prophets and prophecy to his young member, or else believe and expect God to do what was prophesied He would do. So he believed God and was established in his faith for fulfillment; he believed God's prophets and prospered in his ministry.

This testimony is typical of numerous ones from those who have been ministered to by prophets and prophetic presbyteries with similar results. I remind our seminar participants quite often that we do not lay empty hands on empty vessels for empty results, but anointed hands on anointed heads for anointed results. We expect gifts to be imparted and activated within those present at the CI seminars, just as Billy Graham expects the gift of eternal life to be imparted and activated within those who attend his campaigns. The same Gospel truth he preaches that brings faith and conviction for receiving the gift of eternal life is the word of faith we preach that brings the anointing and faith to activate the gifts and callings of God within God's people.

Yet another testimony of the prophetic power to activate ministry comes from the leader of a singing group who ministered with me at a meeting in Atlanta, Georgia, in October 1979. I prophesied to all of his group at this meeting. Part of the prophecy to this young man was that God was giving him the ability to write songs, and these songs would be sung around the world.

He testifies that just a few months after that prophecy, the song "I Am" was birthed within him. That was just the first of many songs he has written since that time. The anointed prophetic word by the prophet was a seed that was planted, and the prophetic anointing awakened that greater ability within him.

That musician kept watering the seed by prayer, by meditation, and by faithfully moving in his ministry until the seed germinated, sprouted, and grew from an anointing in his spirit into a revelation in his mind which brought understanding for the words and music for the song. He has so faithfully cultivated that plant that now he has harvested hundreds of new songs and choruses that are blessing the Body of Christ around the world. By responding properly to his personal prophecy, he has caused every word to come to pass.

A Common Practice in the Early Church. Impartation and activation of ministry was a common practice in the early Church. We can see this in Paul's words to Timothy: *"Neglect not the gift which is in thee, which **was given thee by prophecy**, with the laying on of hands of the presbytery."* Paul was reminding Timothy that his divine gift was imparted to him by prophecy (1 Tim. 4:14). He reminded him again in his second letter to *"stir up the gift of God, which is in thee by the putting on of my hands"* (2 Tim. 1:6). Evidently the apostle believed in and practiced the ministry of laying on of hands and prophecy for the impartation and activation of divine gifts and ministries within God's people. This is confirmed by Paul's statement to the Roman Christians that he longed to be with them, *"that I may impart unto you some spiritual gift, to the end ye may be established"* (Rom. 1:11b).

These Scriptures are sufficient to show us that this practice was a normal, established ministry in the Church. There are in fact as many Scriptures on this subject as on other basic Christian practices, such as communion, water baptism, tithing, offerings, church choir, and orchestra, or the order for a church service. We have clear references in the Epistles and examples in Acts concerning laying on of hands and prophecy for impartation, activation, healing, Holy Spirit direction, revelation, general instruction, and encouragement. In addition, we must also remember that *"laying on of hands"* is one of the six major doctrines of Christ listed in Hebrews 6:1-2.

The churches and individual Christians who do not practice this ministry or have it made available to them are missing a vital work of the Holy Spirit. Scripture tells us that the Spirit is to bring illumination, show us things to come, reveal ministry, and activate gifts. And the prophet and personal prophecy are instruments and avenues by which the Holy Spirit does this part of His work.

CHAPTER 7

PUTTING PERSONAL PROPHECY IN PERSPECTIVE

Christian ministers and church members are faced with making decisions all of their lives. Dedicated Christians want to make their decisions in the will of God. They want every action and attitude in perfect harmony with Heaven.

The Bible gives clear instructions for the general directions and standards for our lives. But how do we make decisions about particular matters for which the Bible cannot give us specific guidance? Take for example the single Christian man who likes two different single Christian women. Both meet all the biblical requirements for a wife, but he cannot marry both of them. He wants God's specific word and will on the matter. So how does he determine the right choice?

Personal prophecy can play an important role in helping believers make decisions of this sort. You may ask, "But is it proper—is it scriptural—for an individual Christian to go to a prophet and expect to receive a specific prophetic word of direction, instruction, or confirmation?" The answer is yes. The Bible provides numerous examples of people, especially those in leadership, going to a prophet and asking for a "thus saith the Lord" about a particular situation.

Specifically, God's people in the Old Testament often sought the high priest for an answer about God's specific will through the Urim and Thummim. These were regularly used by the ancient priest to give a yes or no answer from God to the inquirer. I believe that the New Testament prophet has been given the equivalent of the Urim and Thummim of the Old Testament.

God approves of this practice as long as we do not allow personal prophecy to become a substitute for our seeking God for ourselves through prayer, fasting, and searching the Scriptures. The prophet and personal prophecy are not to take the place of the inner voice of the Holy Spirit within New Testament saints. Instead, they are an extension of the Holy Spirit's ministry of communicating the mind of Christ to individual members of the Body of Christ.

I believe it is just as legitimate scripturally for ministers and saints to seek insight, confirmation, and direction from a prophet about the specifics of God's will as it is to seek directive counseling from a pastor. The pastor will normally use biblical principles and Scriptures to direct the person. He will sometimes insist emphatically, "I do not believe this is the will of God for you" by applying the *Logos* to a specific situation like marriage, business, ministry, or a geographic move.

The prophet, however, will pull from the *Logos* within him and give a *rhema* word to the individual that will answer his questions. A mature prophet who is not personally involved in the situation can even give the mind of Christ on the matter without allowing his personal convictions or theology to influence his answer. Often, in fact, a person asks for a word without even revealing what the matter is. Yet the prophet's anointing (which would be called a word of knowledge or wisdom in the saint) allows him to zero in on the problem with specific insight into the counsel and purpose of God in the matter.

Some years ago, as my reputation as a prophet began to spread, ministers and saints began to call me for a word of the Lord on specific situations. People would also ask questions when I was ministering in personal prophecy at a local church. At first I was afraid to respond, lacking confidence that I had the right to expect God to give me an answer for them.

So I made a thorough search of the Scripture and discovered that it was in fact the prophet's prerogative to ask God for such information. But I also found that God would not give me a specific answer to just any and every request. The law of Moses gave specific instructions about most human relations, and general principles for doing what is right in the sight of God. The law was to be consulted first.

Prophecy is not a play toy or a way to satisfy curiosity. I have found that God will not answer questions that can be resolved by diligently seeking the Scripture. Nor will the Christ within the prophet respond positively when insincere requests are made, or foolish questions are asked.

People often came to Jesus with specific questions. When the query was from a Pharisee, Sadducee, or skeptical lawyer, the motives were usually not pure. So Jesus would answer with another question, a parable, or a brief statement without explanation that sounded like double-talk. On the other hand, those who faithfully followed Him and asked appropriate questions received a clear and compassionate answer.

Sometimes people have asked me inappropriate questions whose answers, even if they could be received from Heaven, would be better off unspoken. Some have said, for example, "My son died two years ago in a car accident; is he in Heaven or hell?" "My house burned six years ago; was it an accident or arsonist?" Young teens have often asked me to describe the person they would marry.

If the answers to these questions were unpleasant, the prophet would not be wise to reveal them even if he knew them. Would the mother really want to know that her son went straight to hell and was suffering eternal torment? Would the teen really like to know that she will grow old without ever being married? No—Jesus wants us to live by faith, with hope and expectancy for His very best and highest in our lives.

We were not designed with the capability to know much about our future; it short-circuits our system's ability to live victoriously and carefree in the present. Jesus taught that each day has enough of its own problems and challenges, and so we should take no thought for tomorrow. Normally God reveals prophetically only those things about the future that we need to know in order to make proper preparation.

Some things, for example, would be edifying to know, or could provide us with a needed release. At one of our Prophets' seminars a woman asked a question at the end of her session with the prophetic presbytery: "My husband," she said, "has been an MIA for 17 years. Could you tell me whether he is alive or dead? I have come to the place that I must know. I have sought the Lord for years, fasting, praying, but I cannot get a clear answer."

The Christ compassion and prophet anointing within me responded, "His spirit is no longer in his mortal body." This dear Christian sister was immediately released in her spirit; her anguish and confusion dissipated and she entered into the peace of God. I do not know why the Lord wanted her answered in that manner. And I am glad she did not ask whether he went to Heaven or hell, because I could not tell by the words or impressions in my spirit. If she had asked, I would have had to say simply, "The Lord is not showing that to me." But the information she did receive was of great benefit to her.

The ministry of the prophet that was in Christ, and that enabled Him to give specific answers to questions that could not be answered by the Scriptures alone, has been invested in the prophets of the Church. Some may ask, "But where are your New Testament examples to verify that claim? Where are the incidents where people came to the prophet and received specific answers to questions?" I would answer that there are as many examples in the New Testament of prophets giving specific prophetic directions to individuals about personal matters as there are of pastors giving counsel to individuals about the same matters.

No texts in the New Testament state or even suggest that a Church prophet does not have all the ministry rights of the prophets of old as well as the Christ-prophet-anointing gift and grace. If the New Covenant does not do away with certain practices or ministries available in the Old, then they are still available in the Church Age. All the Law and Prophets were fulfilled in Jesus. When He ascended into Heaven, He gave the prophets back to the Church—and all that Jesus gave in the New Covenant is better than that in the Old Covenant. Jesus gave prophets to the Church, and they have all the rights and privileges of the Old Covenant, and more.

Yes, then, it is scriptural for a person to go to a prophet, having faith that God will supernaturally meet his need. You can ask questions and expect an answer. But your motives, your attitude, and your question must be proper to receive positive results.

For that reason, you should not go to a prophet until you are sure the Lord is first in your life. You should seek Him, pray, search the Scriptures, and listen for a *rhema* from the Lord until you believe you have an answer. Then, when you go before the prophet, you will be spiritually prepared to respond properly.

Instead of hearing totally new revelation from the prophet, you will then be more likely to hear mostly confirmation of what has already been birthed in your spirit. Such confirmation will give you greater confidence in your ability to hear from God yourself, and will cause you to receive the word in faith, thereby activating the power for the fulfillment of that word.

When you ask the prophet for an answer, the Lord will cause him to respond in one of several ways. If it is a simple yes-or-no question, God will inspire him to give a straight yes or no, or a yes with certain stipulations, or a "God does not want you to know the answer right now, so wait!" If you are seeking insight into ministry through submitting to a prophetic presbytery or going before the prophet, you will probably receive

enough prophecy to fill several pages about you and your ministry potential. Later chapters in this book will help you learn
what to do with the prophecy once you have received it.

Chapter 8

Personal Prophecies Concerning Romance and Marriage

God built within the male and female the desire and potential for romance, love, and marriage. God's natural design is the mutual attraction of man and woman to each other. But Christians need more than a physical attraction and soulish compatibility. There must also be unity of spiritual call and ministry for full compatibility. The highest consideration for the dedicated Christian should be, "Is it the will of God?"

Romantic love and mutual desire between a Christian boy and girl is not conclusive evidence that it is the will of God for them to marry. The decision for marriage needs the "three W's" of the Word, will, and way of God to be fully manifested before marriage is consummated (Chapter 9). The Word of God definitely says that marriage is ordained of God, so it is not difficult to have that light turn green.

The second green light of the will, however, is more difficult to determine. Of the multitude of lovely young Christian ladies, a Christian man must settle with one and be faithful to her. But which one? If mutual attraction and romantic love are not guaranteed proof of the will of God, then how shall he determine which prospect is the perfect will of God? Numerous books have been written on this subject and are available through Christian bookstores. Yet most of these books do not tell how personal prophecy can help determine the will of God in romance and marriage.

We said earlier that in the broad sense, personal prophecy is any method God uses to reveal His specific will to an individual, whether by divinely directed desire, illumination, revelation, vision, or dream. In this discussion of romance and marriage, *"rhema"* will be our general term to refer to all of these means of God communicating His specific will to an individual. The term "prophecy" or "personal prophecy" will refer more specifically to a message conveyed as the will of God through the channel of another person. In this area especially, that distinction is important.

In my personal experience in counseling hundreds of young people in Bible college, as well as prophesying over thousands of singles in churches throughout the world, I have found that romance, love, and marriage are the most dangerous areas for receiving personal prophecies from others. This is evidently a touchy subject with the Lord. Rarely will the Holy Spirit use *personal prophecy* to activate romance and bring direction as to who should marry whom. But each Christian considering marriage needs a personal *rhema* from the Lord to bring assurance and peace concerning his or her mate.

Guidelines for Prophetic Romances and Marriages. One certain prophetic rule for romance and marriage is that the Holy Spirit works on *both* parties. I have counseled numerous young women and men who thought the Lord had told them they were to marry a certain person, but the other party had no mutual desire, leading, or inclination. Whenever one person thinks he or she has a *rhema*—or someone has given that person a prophecy—about marrying a certain other person, if the other person has sensed nothing along that line, then usually it is not a true word from the Lord. There are occasions when one person will know it is the will of God a few weeks or months before the other. But when that is the case, the knowing party must wait until the way of the Lord works it out.

Every unmarried pastor who has a congregation with several single young ladies is plagued by two particular problems. One is that most of the older women are trying to play Cupid, and the "spooky spirituals" are getting "revelations" about the woman he is to marry. Meanwhile, the younger single women begin receiving what I call "wishions"—that is, wishful thinking which they call divine visions.

I pastored as a single person for two years, and during that time several young ladies received "wishions" that I was to be their husband. Each was convinced that she had received a vision or direct word from the Lord. Yet the young lady who became my wife never once felt she had received anything from the Lord to marry me prior to my telling her I loved her and asking her to marry me. She felt God had spoken to her in her early years that she would marry a preacher, but she did not jump to any conclusions just because I was her pastor and single.

Once a couple has mutually agreed that they love each other and are seriously praying about marriage, then confirmation concerning the will of God should be sought from pastoral counseling and prophetic confirmation from a mature, proven prophet. This is one area where prophecy should be a confirmation and not a revelation. Of course, God will not always give a confirmation through the means we desire, but He will give us the peace, assurance, and faith we need to know that it is His will, and to make a successful marriage.

Let me illustrate this insight with a personal experience. After I had decided that Evelyn was the young lady I loved and wanted to marry, and had confirmed it by every way I could find, a date was set for the wedding. But I had been exposed to several ladies who had "wishions" about a helpmate, and to statements by preachers and Christian authors that a wife could make or break the minister, and make life heaven on earth or hell on earth. So I felt I had to know it was the perfect will of God before I married. I knew I loved her, but I wanted to make sure she was the right one for me and for the ministry God had ordained for my life.

I had once been engaged to a preacher's daughter when I was in Bible college, and that had proved not to be the will of God. So that experience also contributed to a fearful obsession to know beyond a shadow of a doubt that Evelyn was the perfect mate for me, and that she was ordained of God.

The wedding date was set for August 13, 1955. We were scheduled to attend a conference in Canada where they believed in prophecy and provided prophetic presbytery for those whom they felt led to call forth. So I started fasting before we went to the conference. The fast extended for nine days. I was so serious that I wrote the Lord a prayer letter, reminding Him that He promised that whatsoever I asked in His name, that would He do. I told Him I wanted the prophets to call me forth and prophesy, "Yea, My son, the one you have chosen is the one I have ordained for you...fear not...it's My perfect will."

The conference had two services a day for seven days in the middle of July. I prayed for hours at a time that week, and continued fasting the whole time, but not once did they call me forth for prophetic presbytery, nor did anyone give me a word privately. Since I was scheduled to be married within three weeks of returning to my pastorate in Washington, I had to know it was God's will.

Surely, I reasoned, God is as concerned as I am—so why doesn't He speak to me through the prophet or prophetic presbytery? I had pressed God for a vision, dream, angelic visitation, or some means of supernatural confirmation and had received none. Personal prophecy was now my last chance for a supernatural confirmation before my marriage date, but those prophesying did not even look my way.

As it turned out, God had His own way to answer my prayer. The main speaker at the conference had a dynamic ministry in the Word. He preached such simplicity of faith and trust in God during that conference that by the end, faith, assurance, and peace had been birthed in my heart. God did not give supernatural confirmation to my marriage by any of the ways I had suggested and strongly requested, but He did do it by a *rhema* from the preaching of the *Logos* of God.

My wife and I have been married now for 32 years, and we have had the most compatible and fulfilling marriage of any couple we have known or have counseled. We must trust God to reveal His will and bring confirmation to major decisions such as marriage, but we must not try to force God to do it one particular way. Our attitude should be one of faith in God as a person with a loving, trustworthy nature, and the power to fulfill our prayers and bring revelation and confirmation through many ways—including personal prophecy.

Prophetic Marriages Brought About by Personal Prophecy and *Rhema*

Some marriages I have seen God put together are not the average "boy meets girls—falls in love—long engagement—wedding" type. In all of our years of ministry, I personally know of less than a dozen marriages that have been activated and brought together by the supernatural rather than the natural methods of romance and marriage.

The method of marriage by the arrangement of the Father is not altogether unusual. The modern Western way of romance and marriage is not the way it was done in Bible days. Fathers made arrangements for the marriages, and many times the bride and bridegroom never even met until the wedding night. Typical of such a marriage was that of Isaac and Rebekah, which was strictly arranged by Abraham (a type of God) and Eliezer (a type of the Holy Spirit).

God, our heavenly Father, still makes special arrangements for some marriages without following the natural path of dating, romantic love, romance, and marriage. But when God arranges such a marriage, it works better in the long run than those which result from just natural attraction and soulish motivation. Our heavenly Father knows what is best for His children, even in matching them for marriage.

Romance and Marriage With Prophetic Involvement. An example of a prophetic marriage is that of a couple we have known for years. The man had been saved out of the drug culture, and God had called him to ministry. At the time this incident took place, he was associate pastor of a church in Orlando, Florida.

The woman was one of his church members. Her husband, a major in the Army, had been killed in action, so she was left a widow with four small children. The pastor had visited her several times on his visitation rounds.

After several days of fasting and prayer about his future, including marriage, the pastor received a *rhema* on a Saturday morning that he was to marry this widow. He asked the Lord when they were to get married, and the word came back that it should happen on the following Thursday.

Before this time, neither of them had ever entertained any thoughts of romance toward each other, let alone marriage. So when this young pastor called the woman to tell her what he thought the Lord had said to him, she told him he was crazy. She had no intention of marrying him, especially not in four days! The pastor said that the Lord told him she was supposed to go in her closet and pray. She rejected the word and hung up the phone, but then thought it would not hurt to go in her closet and pray. When she kneeled in her closet, she looked up—and there was the wedding dress she had bought a few days before, just because it was so beautiful and on such a good sale. She had said, "If I ever get married again, this is the dress I want to be married in."

The Lord spoke to her clearly and said: "I was the one who inspired you to buy that dress so you would have it for your wedding Thursday." So they were married that Thursday, and have had a very successful marriage and ministry together. The two older children have graduated from Oral Roberts University, and this couple is pastoring a successful church in

California and conducting Prophets' conferences throughout the United States.

One final example of prophetic marriage illustrates that when a prophetic word is truly from the Lord, it will come to pass regardless of seeming impossibilities. My wife's baby sister, Sharon, was three years old when she served as flower girl at our wedding. Fifteen years later, on August 25, 1970, we were praying for Sharon at the church we all attended in San Antonio, Texas. I prophesied to her that day, and one part of the prophecy said her wedding plans would be settled within one year. She was 18 years old.

The following July my wife told me Sharon was counting on that prophecy coming to pass. The year would be up within six weeks. At the time, Sharon and her parents were going back to North Carolina to visit some friends. She hoped to get together with her boyfriend who was stationed at an army base in the same state. Because of the prophecy, we expected that they would become engaged while she was there.

When Sharon arrived back the first week of August, however, to our surprise she had broken up with her boyfriend altogether. But the following Sunday she was playing the piano at church. Six soldiers were there from Fort Sam Houston, and one of them felt the Lord spoke to him that the girl playing the piano was the wife God had ordained for him.

They dated a few times during the next two weeks, and on August 24, they were in my office for counsel about marriage. The next night they met with her parents and her wedding plans were settled, exactly one year from the date the prophecy was given that her wedding plans would be settled within one year. I teasingly tell my brother-in-law that God sent him along to marry Sharon to retain my reputation as a true prophet.

We should note again emphatically that these prophetically motivated marriages are the exception to the rule, and not the standard for Christians. I know many saints who thought they had received a rhema from the Lord that they were to marry a certain person, but it proved to be their own wishful thinking and imagination. In other chapters of this book we offer many guidelines for determining whether a thought is a true *rhema* from the Lord. The main criterion in prophetic marriages, however, is that *both* parties must be dealt with by the Lord, and both must come to mutual agreement without one putting undue pressure on the other.

My advice to unmarried Christians is to refrain from asking for a prophetic romance and marriage—but if that is how God moves supernaturally, then do not be afraid of it. There must, however, be a *rhema* within both parties. One party cannot make it on the conviction and revelation of the other if there is no witness or birthing of the Holy Spirit within his or her own heart. A person should never feel compelled to enter into a relationship with another if he or she does not feel the same nor receive the same *rhema* after earnestly and sincerely seeking God about the matter.

We must remember that God's natural process for marriage is mutual attraction, romance, friendship, love, mutual witness of the Holy Spirit, pastoral counseling and parental consent, and then wisdom and providential timing for the date of marriage. There are a few exceptions to the natural process, and there are some supernatural prophetic marriages, but God is the one who determines which way He will bring a man and woman together whom He has ordained to be husband and wife.

CHAPTER 9

DISCOVERING GOD'S WORD, WILL, AND WAY

Though personal prophecy can play an important role in helping Christians make decisions, it is by no means the only way the Holy Spirit uses to reveal God's will and way. In my 33 years of ministry, I have had to make thousands of major and minor decisions. The major decisions, like marriage and ministry, have been so critical to the direction of my life that I have wanted to know beyond any shadow of a doubt that they were in the perfect will of God.

In this decision-making process, personal prophecy has played a part; but it has not been dominant. Probably 90 percent of my decisions have been made without personal prophecy being the dominating or even motivating factor. But I have striven to make one hundred percent of all my decisions to be based upon God's Word, will, and way. A discussion of these factors can clarify when, where, and to what extent personal prophecy is to function in our lives.

The most accurate method of making sure you do everything in harmony with Heaven is to follow the "Three W's" of decision making: Determine God's *Word* on a matter, His specific *will* about it, and His *way* to fulfill it. These are like three traffic lights that must all be "green" before we can proceed on our way.

The normal procedure is to make sure you have a "go" on the number one traffic light of the Word. If it is red (no), don't go any further. If it is green, go on to the next light of God's will. Stay put until it is green as well; a yellow (take caution; no definite yes or no yet) means wait. Finally, when the third light of God's way is green, you can proceed at the proper speed. You now have the mind and timing of the Lord, so finalize the decision and take immediate action.

The third light is especially important. Most sincere Christians are diligent to act according to the Word of God, and they are willing to seek His will on a matter. But they are not always faithful to wait until God's way is made clear.

A closer look at each of these traffic lights will help us see how they allow us to determine the mind of Christ, walk by faith, be led by the Spirit, put personal prophecy in its place, and fulfill our personal rhema from the Lord.

The Word

The Bible is the highest authority and has the final say in all matters. It is the revelation of God in written form as Jesus was the revelation of God in human form. The Scripture contains the thoughts, desires, and purposes of God revealed and written for all to read and understand.

This Book of Heaven was inspired by the Holy Spirit and given to men so that they can fulfill the prayer petition, *"Thy kingdom come, Thy will be done, on earth as it is in heaven."* It contains the do's and don'ts of what is good and bad, right and wrong, for all mankind, and especially for Christians. Rightly understood, the Bible is consistent with itself from Genesis to Revelation.

For a person to receive a green light on the Word, he must have more than just one obscure verse for authorization. It must be part of the *Logos* and not just a *rhema* found in the Bible but intended for someone else. We cannot use the *rhema* to Isaiah to go naked in public, or the *rhema* to Hosea to marry a harlot, in order to justify our doing the same thing today. The personal prophecies of biblical figures or of our contemporaries cannot be used to establish doctrine or become a pattern for all to follow. Thus we must go to the Bible, not with the desire to legitimize our desires, but rather to submit them to the Word of God and have them come in line with the *Logos*.

Before the green light of the Word can come on, the spirit of the Word and the letter of the Word must agree. God is Spirit, and the spirit of the Word is the nature, character, and principles of God. You may think you have found a verse or two that gives you a green light, but if it is contrary to the nature of God, and His general principles, then you are misinterpreting the verse and taking it out of context.

A minister once came to me and said he had received a *"rhema"* from the Lord that he was to leave his wife. She had become discouraged and resentful, and was refusing to travel with him in the ministry or be involved in pastoral work. She had become a weight of resistance and was causing him to "sin" against God by not fulfilling his preaching ministry. He was convinced that the Lord had spoken to him the Scriptures *"Lay aside every weight, and the sin which doth so easily beset us,"* and he that leaves *"...wife...for My sake, and the gospel's"* will be blessed (Heb. 12:1b; Mark 10:29b).

I did not prophesy to him; instead I gave him prophetic pastoral counseling. I told him that it was not the will and the way of God for him to divorce his wife, though he seemed to have some Scriptures that justified his desire. He argued that souls were dying and going to hell, and thousands of people were not being ministered to, because they were being denied his preaching and healing ministry. If he could just get rid of the weight of his wife, he said, he would be free to move in his ministry. He insisted that he was greatly burdened for Christ's Bride, the Church, and he wanted to minister to her.

A year later I was back in his area and met him again, so I inquired about his marital status. He said he had prayed much about it and considered all the hours of counsel that had been given him. While he was praying one day, beseeching the Lord to release him from his wife so he could minister to the Church, the Lord spoke to him clearly and emphatically a true *rhema* which settled the issue for him. Christ Jesus told him, "If you cannot minister love, life, and restoration to your own bride, do you think I want to turn you loose on Mine?" So he put his heart into loving and restoring his wife, and they are together in the ministry today.

Expose every thought, impression, and suggestion that comes to you from any source—regardless of how spiritual or religious it may sound—to the whole Bible. To avoid entering into deception and delusion, keep a love for the truth as it is, and not what you selfishly want to interpret it to be. Let the Word of God (*Logos*) dispel and destroy all self-delusion of the deceitful heart. Only the two-edged sword of the Word of God can divide soul and spirit and reveal whether the thought and impression comes from the soulish realm or the spiritual one.

Thoughts and desires should not be made prayer petitions until they receive a green light from the Word. If your thought or desire is unscriptural, improper, illegal, or immoral according to divine principles, then you are wasting your time asking God to let you do it. God and His Word are one: *"There are three that bear record in heaven, the Father, the Word, and the Holy Ghost: and these three are one"* (1 John 5:7).

The Holy Spirit will never tell you to do something contrary to the nature of God or the Holy Scriptures. Heaven will not answer such petitions. Any contrary thought that seems to be an answer to your prayers and meditation would have to come from soulish imagination, selfish deception, or the devil. Peter declared that it is possible to take Scripture out of context and twist it to one's own deception and destruction (2 Pet. 3:16). This is precisely what has been done by cultic groups such as the Jehovah's Witnesses and the Mormons.

True, conscientious Christians cannot have faith to receive the answers to their prayers unless they are confident that what they are asking is the will of God for them: *"And this is the confidence that we have in Him, that, if we ask any thing according to His will, He heareth us: and if we know that He hear us...we know that we have the petitions that we desired of Him"* (1 John 5:14-15). If you know your petition is scripturally the will of God, then you will have confidence and faith to believe God for it.

For that reason, before you accept any thought as from the Lord, or embark upon any enterprise, make sure you have an absolute green light from the Word of God, the Bible. But even then, you do not yet have an open road for full speed ahead. You must look for two more traffic lights before you can have Heaven's full approval, authority, and anointing.

The Will of God

Just as God has a general will for all mankind, He also has a specific will for individuals. He has general directives for the corporate Body of Christ, and specific directions for the individual members of that Body. Just as all directions for the human body come from the head, all directives for the Body of Christ—both corporate and individual—come from Christ Jesus, the Head of the Church.

All true *rhemas* and leadings of the Spirit will be in harmony with God's overall purposes, and for the edification of the whole Body of Christ. But just as the human head's directives to the eye are not the same as those for the ear or any other part, Christ's specific will and instructions for each member and ministry in the Body are not all the same. They must be personalized by individual application.

For that reason, the Bible can only give general directions to the whole Body of Christ, a few qualifications and requirements for certain ministries, and a general description of what to do. Without the working of the Holy Spirit and Christ's fivefold ministry—especially the prophet—the Bible cannot by itself provide specific directions and reveal the will of God concerning all personal matters.

The Bible declares, for example, *"Go ye into all the world, and preach the gospel to every creature"* (Mark 16:15b). The Holy Spirit is today raising up a great army of Christian soldiers to fulfill this commission. Now suppose that a dedicated Christian wants to be a part of that fulfillment as a true soldier of the cross. In which "division" of the Lord's army does he enlist: the preaching division, the praying division, or the paying division who support it? Is he to go into full-time ministry? If so, does he preach in his homeland or in a foreign land? Or is he to be a Christian businessman who provides the means to finance the frontline preaching division? Or is it perhaps God's will for him to be a part of the great intercessory prayer division? Every "soldier" is called to do some of all three of these activities, but we must major in one to be effective; and we need to know God's will about our "major."

The Bible gives general criteria for making many decisions in business, travel, ministry, and use of our finances. But it does not provide many specifics. Scripture says that it is not good for a man to be alone, and that marriage is honorable; but it does not specify which saintly woman to marry. Mutual attraction and romantic feelings between a Christian man and woman are no guarantee that it is God's will for them to marry. And just because a business endeavor is legal and scriptural does not mean that it is God's will for an individual to be involved in it. God's specific will never contradicts His general will, but it may sometimes supersede His general will.

Jesus prayed in the Garden of Gethsemane, "Father...not My will but Thine be done." David, the king after God's own heart, prayed, "Teach me to do Thy will...O God." The Father had a specific will for Jesus that others could not fulfill. He had a specific role for David as for all the other godly patriarchs, kings, and prophets.

So how do we come to know the specific will of God for our lives? We must take a look at the ways God made His will known to people in the Bible, and then see how the Holy Spirit works with saints today to reveal His specific will for them.

God's methods of personal, individual revelation in the Scripture were widely varied. He directed Joseph by dreams. He spoke to Moses with an audible voice out of the fire. He whispered to Elijah in a still, small voice. He sent the archangel Gabriel to Mary. He appeared personally to Paul in the glorified body of Jesus. He spoke to David through the prophecy of Samuel and Nathan. He sent word to Jehu through the prophet Elisha and others. He directed Timothy through the laying on of hands with prophecy by the presbytery. And He guided Jesus through divine revelation knowledge.

Given all these ways of discovering God's will, we need some guidelines and safeguards for discerning it in our own lives. Once we have passed the traffic light of God's Word and are assured that what we are considering is in keeping with both the context and the spirit of the Word, we can expect the Holy Spirit by the following biblical methods to bring clarity, assurance, and direction.

God's Method for Revealing His Perfect Will

Divinely Directed Desire. The psalmist said, *"I delight to do Thy will, O my God"* (Ps. 40:8). God's greatest delight is for His children to desire to do His will—to take delight willingly in crucifying the flesh and fulfilling the desires of the Holy Spirit. He takes no pleasure in pressuring His children to do His will.

God's Word assures us that if we delight ourselves in the Lord, He will give us the desires of our heart (Ps. 37:4). This Scripture, I believe, has a twofold application. First, it means that God will cause us to desire what He wants us to have. Second, as we trust in Him, He will cause that prophetically inspired desire to come to pass. Consequently, desire can be a supernatural indication of the will of God. But desire alone, without additional confirmations, is insufficient evidence for concluding that what we desire is the perfect will of God.

Rhema and Scripture Illumination

A *rhema* is an inspired word birthed within your own spirit, a whisper from the Holy Spirit like the still, small voice that spoke to Elijah in the cave (1 Kings 19). It is a divinely inspired impression upon your soul, a flash of thought or a creative idea from God. It is conceived in your spirit, but birthed into your natural understanding by divine illumination. A true *rhema* carries with it a deep inner assurance and witness of the Spirit.

God sometimes reveals His will by a *rhema* from "out of the clear blue." But at other times we receive it by an illumination of a particular Scripture. As we read, God sends a quickening *rhema* that says, "This applies to you."

Jesus received direction for His ministry that way (Luke 4:16-21). This type of divine directive may also be called "revelation knowledge" or "scriptural illumination."

The Prophet and Personal Prophecy

God still uses the prophet today to give specific, directive words to the saints about their personal lives. These directive prophecies are not usually given through someone moving in the gift of prophecy, but rather through the prophet. Though saints and other ministers may receive a word of knowledge or wisdom on a matter, a "thus saith the Lord" with specific, directive words should usually come from the office of the prophet.

This is true because the word of a mature, proven prophet with a track record of being accurate can be taken seriously, evaluated, and acted upon immediately. We should always consider carefully any prophetic word given to us, whatever its source. But when a person without a proven ministry gives me a word, and I do not relate to it or have a clear witness to it, then I usually wait for more confirmation through several human vessels before I act on it. The only words I reject completely are those which are unscriptural or are clearly not from God.

Many areas of major ministry in my life were first planted in my spirit or brought to light by personal prophecy. I believe that this ministry within the Church will increase and become more prominent as God's great company of prophets are manifested.

The Gifts of the Holy Spirit

The Holy Spirit can make known the specific will of God through His nine gifts, especially the "revelation gifts" of the word of knowledge and the word of wisdom. Ministers and businessmen need desperately to know how to allow these gifts to make wise decisions in their churches and businesses. Parents need these gifts for making family decisions when natural knowledge is insufficient and the Bible is not specific.

A choice between right or wrong is not difficult for a dedicated Christian. But when the choice is between two right things, supernatural help is needed. The gifts of the Spirit are available for every Christian, to help us discover God's will on matters and to follow through with wise decisions.

The Fruits of the Holy Spirit

To be led by the Holy Spirit does not mean that we are led only by supernatural manifestations of the gifts. The supernatural fruits of the Spirit are just as vital in determining the mind of Christ as the gifts. The fruits and gifts are like two sides of the same coin, and both sides must be in good shape for it to be "spendable."

Evangelicals tend to emphasize the fruits of the Spirit, and charismatics the gifts. But the Holy Spirit is not in competition with Himself. Both the fruits and the gifts are manifestations of the Spirit's activity in our lives.

Isaiah declared prophetically, *"You shall go out with **joy**, and be led forth with **peace**"* (Isa. 55:12a, emphasis added). To make decisions according to the spiritual peace they bring is being led by the Spirit. To take action because of the joy of the Lord is to be motivated by the Holy Spirit. To move in faith—which is both a gift and a fruit of the Spirit—is moving in the mind of Christ and walking with God, *"For we walk by faith, not by sight"* (2 Cor. 5:7).

Of these, the peace of God is particularly important. Paul declared that the spiritual mind can be identified by the extent of its life and peace: *"to be spiritually minded is **life** and **peace**"* (Rom. 8:6b). He also instructed us to let the peace of Christ rule—that is, govern and direct—our hearts (Col. 3:15), for God's peace should override all confusion, doubt, and indecision: *"The peace of God, which passeth all understanding, shall keep your hearts and minds through Christ Jesus"* (Phil. 4:7). If you want to know the specific will of God, *"Depart from evil, and do good; seek **peace**, and pursue it"* (Ps. 34:14, emphasis added).

In determining the will of God on a matter, then, look inside your soul and spirit to see how much peace and joy you have about the situation. How many of the nine fruits of the Spirit are evident in the matter? Do you have faith or doubt, love or fear, desire or dread, joy or anxiety, peace or pressure, meekness or self-determination, temperance or impatience? If you have the mind of Christ on the matter and are being led by the Spirit, you will find the right fruits within. If you do not have them, then the traffic light of God's will has not turned green. Do nothing, make no commitments or final decisions, until this light gives you the go-ahead.

The Witness, Clearance, or Restraint of the Holy Spirit

The apostle Paul did not always know exactly what the Lord wanted him to do. So if he was unable to find out supernaturally which way to go for ministry, he would simply go the way he thought best. If the Holy Spirit did not want him to go to that place at that time, He would give Paul a check or restraint in his own spirit.

The incidents in Acts 15 and 16 show the apostle operating this way when he intended to preach in Asia, but was rerouted by the Lord instead to Macedonia. These events prove that God has a general will as well as a specific will. It was His general will for the Gospel to be preached to every creature, but He had specific plans for when, where, and how it should be preached.

To know and follow God's will for our lives, then, we must be very sensitive to the checks and restraints of the Holy Spirit. He will also *"bear witness with our spirit"* (Rom. 8:16b) to help us know His mind. The prophet Agabus, for example, gave Paul a prophecy that he was going to face suffering and prison in Jerusalem. The brethren tried to talk him out of going, but he went on, because the revelation was nothing new to him. The Spirit had been witnessing to the same truth in almost every city on his journey (Acts 20:22; 21:1-14). Agabus's prophecy was just another confirmation of what had been said in numerous personal prophecies given to him before.

If you want the green light of God's will to shine, then you must have clearance in your spirit. Never ignore promptings or restraints from the Holy Spirit; it will dull your spiritual senses. It will also change God's ordained green light into a blinking yellow light inside that causes you to become either self-willed and set in your ways, or else bound up in a perpetual state of confusion and indecision.

Wise Counsel

One of the biblical names for Jesus is "Counselor" (Isa. 9:6). It reveals His nature and character as One who reveals His will and way through counseling. His name is also "Everlasting Father" and "Good Shepherd," because pastoral and parental counseling—godly advice from those wiser and more mature than ourselves—is an important way of determining the will of God.

Numerous Scriptures confirm the necessity of seeking counsel before making major decisions: *"He that harkeneth unto counsel is wise." "Where no counsel is, the people fall: but in the multitude of counsellors there is safety." "Plans go wrong with too few counsellors; many counsellors bring success." "Hear counsel, and receive instruction, that thou mayest be wise in thy latter end." "There are many devices in a man's heart; nevertheless, the counsel of the Lord, that shall stand." "Every purpose is established by counsel; and with good advice go to war." "Don't go to war without wise guidance; there is safety in many counsellors"* (Prov. 11:14; 12:15; 15:22; 19:20; 20:18; 24:6). If it is wise to seek counsel in matters of war, how much more so in matters of God's will, which pertains to eternal life and death endeavors?

Seeking counsel is critical, then, but we must seek it with an open heart rather than concluding ahead of time that we know the will of God. When we approach a prophet, pastor, parent, or elder, we should not talk and act as if we already have our minds settled: "God told me to do this, but I was wondering what you think about it." If God really told you to do it, who will be willing to argue with God? That attitude makes it difficult for another person to give you proper counsel. God will not force His counsel on you any more than He forces His salvation on you.

Confirmation

One of the best known principles for determining the will of God is the scriptural requirement that everything must be confirmed in the mouth of two or three witnesses before accepting it as fact. This principle about receiving confirmation was established in the law of Moses (Deut. 17:6; 19:15) and reestablished under grace in the Church by the apostle Paul (2 Cor. 13:1).

The rule can be applied to a word of counsel, a word of prophecy, or a *rhema* word. Just as the general will of God cannot be established by a single verse, neither can the specific will of God be established by one prophecy, one *rhema*, one counselor, or one anything else. It is not offensive to the Lord for you to withhold judgment on a word until you receive confirmation from two or three other sources. In fact, He insists that in all serious matters there be at least two and preferably three witnesses before you accept a prophetic word.

Unity

When more than one party is involved in a decision, agreement and unity among them is essential for God's will to be revealed. When everyone is in the specific will of God, there will be unity. For a husband and wife, for example, to be in full agreement and peace about a matter is indicative of God's will. We must be in unity with God, ourselves, and others who are involved in the decision, and Psalm 133 tells us that where there is unity, there is life.

By now we have accumulated a number of indications of God's will. Suppose we have taken a specific desire and what we believe to be a directive word from the Lord, and exposed it to the whole Word of God, both in Spirit and in context. The Word light has turned green. Then suppose we have received several personal prophecies and proper counsel, which have brought confirmations in the mouth of two or three witnesses. We have the fruit of the Holy Spirit with regard to the matter, and there are no checks or restraints from the Spirit, but rather a sense of peace and clearance. All pertinent parties are in unity; all things are in order.

At this point, we can move in the confidence that it is His general will, based on the Word, and His specific will, based on the confirmed rhema. But these two green lights of Word and will are not enough to act upon. The third light, the way of God, must turn green as well before the work of God can be accomplished.

The Way of the Lord

The Word gives Heaven's authorization, and God's will specifies that a course of action is for you. But you still must know the *way* to fulfill God's desire. The way of God includes His timing, methods, and necessary means to do it; the who, what, when, where, and how (but not always the why); the continued guidance and control of circumstances by God; and the patience to press on until His plan is accomplished.

To possess the way, we need above all *patience*: *"Ye have need of patience, that after you have done the will of God you might receive the* [prophetic] *promise"* (Heb. 6:12). The person with patience will eventually possess the promise.

Sadly enough, most Christians are not even aware of this third traffic light in their walk with God. So many endeavors fail because they were not attempted according to God's way. *"There is a way which seemeth right unto a man, but* [they] *are the ways of death"* (Prov. 14:12). God's ways are not our ways, for they are as much higher than ours as the heavens are high above the earth (Isa. 55:9).

Often God's Word and will are much easier to determine than His way. The Word can be determined by examining a book, the will by personal inward principles and confirmations from others. But the way is a time process that must be walked out day by day, because all the details of it are rarely ever revealed ahead of time.

Certainly, personal prophecies can play a part in revealing the way, giving road signs at critical junctures to point the right direction and to say how long till the next turn. But God is apparently reluctant to give out too many details, and so the way is often worked out in the same way we put together a jigsaw puzzle—one piece at a time. And the individual pieces of the process often fail to make sense in themselves, only gaining significance when the overall picture has finally come in sight.

God's Way for Abraham and Moses

We can see this process illustrated in the lives of Abraham and Moses. First of all, the word of God to Abraham was to leave Ur of the Chaldees, become the father of a great race of people for the Lord, and possess Canaan as homeland and headquarters. This word was spoken as God's specific will through divine revelation, and confirmed by several prophecies.

The way for Abraham to fulfill God's desire was to look and walk the length and breadth of the land (Gen. 13:17). His personal responsibility was to keep looking and walking all the days of his life, and to believe that every place he put his foot within the designated borders would be given to him and his seed for an inheritance. (Note, however, that God's way for Joshua to possess the land four hundred years later was different.)

The particular place God had chosen for possession was Canaan, but the place He designated for the nation to grow was Egypt. The appointed time for the fulfillment of His desire was not until four centuries later, when the land was fully conquered and possessed by Israel. For that reason, patience was critical for Abraham and his seed; they had to wait until the sins of the Amorites had reached their fullness, and his descendants had multiplied to become like the stars of the sky and the sands of the seashore. God's word and will came quickly, but it took hundreds of years for His way to be completely unfolded. God prophetically speaks to nations in relation to centuries, to families in relation to generations, and to individuals according to an entire lifetime.

Moses is a second good example of this process. The word of the Lord came to him to deliver His three million chosen people out of Egyptian bondage, and to take them to the land promised to Abraham. God's specific will was made known by the audible voice of God and confirmed by signs and wonders.

God's *way* for the Israelites was to travel through the two-year wilderness route rather than the eleven-day route, which was the well-traveled road to Canaan. His provision came in the plagues on Egypt, the parting of the Red Sea, and the miracles and manna in the desert. He guided them by the pillar of fire by night and the cloud by day.

The people had to endure patiently until Pharaoh gave the order to release them, and then again in the wilderness. Though the generation of liberated slaves were the specific people God wanted to possess Canaan, they eventually lost patience, sinned, and rebelled. So Joshua and the younger generation fulfilled the prophecy instead.

This meant an extension of their timetable into 40 years of wandering. The people had to follow the cloud and fire until God was ready for them to take Canaan. He wanted sufficient time to put into place everything necessary to fulfill His purposes: a tabernacle to be His dwelling place; a code of laws to preserve them and maintain them in a right relationship with Him and with each other; and a political system to transform them from a disordered multitude into 12 organized tribes arranged in His order around the place of His presence. This training period also gave them enough exposure to enemies to gain a proper training for warfare, and to move at once by faith when the challenge came to enter the land, drive out the giants, and take possession.

Not a Formula, But a Flow of Faith

Joshua had to discover God's unique way for conquering each of the nations he encountered in Israel. Jericho, for example, had to be taken in a peculiar way; and when they simply assumed that they knew how to take the city of Ai, they lost the battle. David also won every battle differently, because he waited for the green light of God's way before venturing into conflict. One time the green light was actually given by the rustling in the tops of the mulberry trees!

We, too, need special wisdom to do the specific will of God. Ministry must be launched in the fullness of time; if the timing is not right, catastrophe can result. Our attitude must also be right. For example, it is God's Word and specific will for us to forgive those who trespass against us. But the way some of us go about it negates its effectiveness: "I want you to forgive me for my honest mistake, and I forgive you for your dumb actions and immature attitude, and pray that you will never be that stupid again."

Our action must also be according to God's often unusual plan. Many times His way is not practical human reasoning; it is not the way natural man would do it. Because God's way is a walk of faith, not by sight, we cannot depend on natural knowledge. We must have divine revelation.

Some people are called to preach and prophesy. But they try to do it by imitating someone else rather than by seeking God's specific way for them. Some Christians receive personal prophecies about great financial prosperity, but they never fulfill it because they never find out God's way to do it. Still others find God's way, but after they start acting according to it, they gradually revert back to their old ways, losing God's anointing upon His will for their lives.

Once the Word has given approval, and the will has been revealed, the way must be waited for until it is made known. We must pray the prayer of the "man after God's own heart," David: *"Teach me thy **way**, O Lord"* (Ps. 27:11a, emphasis added). God said that He showed His *acts* to Israel, but He made known His *ways* to Moses; so we must be like Moses.

God has not only a time for every work under Heaven, but also a right way for it to be accomplished. So the key to successful Christian endeavors is to find His *way* to fulfill His *will* with the authority of His *Word*. With all three traffic lights green, we can proceed at full speed to obey God.

CHAPTER 10

BUSINESS ENDEAVORS AND FINANCIAL PROSPERITY

Rhemas, personal prophecy, and the gifts of the Holy Spirit should certainly be active in the business endeavors and financial prosperity of Christians. Numerous testimonies have been given about supernatural understanding and divinely directed decisions that brought about profitable business deals for ministers and Christian businessmen.

Voice magazine is the official monthly publication of the Full Gospel Business Men's Fellowship International. For years it has published testimonies of men from all walks of life who have not only had supernatural salvation, baptism of the Holy Spirit, healings, and great deliverances, but also a word from the Lord—a *rhema* concerning their business endeavors and financial prosperity. But because of the lack of active, mature prophets in the Church during the last three decades, there have been very few testimonies of prophets giving personal prophecies in this area. This is changing now, and such prophecy will continue to increase more and more as God's great company of prophets keep coming forth in maturity. For the businessman needs the ministry of the prophet to bless his business just as a pastor needs the prophet to establish, bless, and prosper his church.

Pastors and Christian businessmen and women have survived and even prospered without the prophet till now. However, since the Holy Spirit has made known that now is the time for the army of the Lord to arise and possess the wealth of the world, the forces of the enemy have been greatly intensified against Christians who have dedicated their businesses to God for the upbuilding of God's Kingdom. Now we will need greater supernatural assistance to make Christian businesses prosper. New legions of the hordes of hell have been unleashed to stop the financial and material prosperity of the true Church. But the army of the Lord with its Commander in Chief, Jesus Christ, will subdue all the kingdoms of this world under the domain of the Kingdom of God.

Three Army Divisions

The army of the Lord has three divisions: the prophetic-preaching division, the paying-providing division, and the praying-procuring division. Christian businessmen and women make up the paying-providing division. Their division must go into the devil's world of finances and break down the gates of hell to bring forth the finances needed for buildings, transportation, and communication to preach the Gospel of the Kingdom in every nation. Those ministering financial provision desperately need the prophets and intercessory prayer warriors from the other divisions in order to conquer the enemy zone assigned to them by the Holy Spirit. As all three army divisions in the Church work together, the whole creation will finally see that the gates of hell cannot prevail against the Church of the living God.

This truth is one reason why the Church has such a vital need for a book of guidelines for personal prophecy. In order for Christians to appropriate properly for their business the benefits of a prophetic word, they must have a solid understanding of God's prophetic ministry. They need to know what God means when He uses certain terms and phrases in prophetic terminology. They need to know God's ways of bringing prophetic proclamations to pass in the prophetic process. They certainly need to understand God's prophetic timing, which is rarely in line with what we think it must be. So a few truths that are presented in other chapters need to be summarized here.

Prophetic Principles: A Summary

Several prophetic principles operate in all great endeavors which are for God and directed by the Holy Spirit. If you just started reading in this part of the book, or have not studied the biblical examples that portray these principles concerning the characteristics of personal prophecy, then re-read these areas.

1. *Before great personal prophecies come to pass, things nearly always get worse before they get better.*

2. *Delays are not denials, but are designed to bring a dedication of the person to God and of his prosperity to God's purpose.*

3. *Promotion and prosperity come from the Lord for His people.*

4. *The purpose of the divinely planned process for procurement means more to God than the end product, for the maturing of the person means more to God than his financial prosperity.*

5. *Proper biblical success principles must be patiently and persistently practiced in order to produce what has been prophetically promised.*

6. *The "Saul syndrome" of stubbornness, self-deception, self-justification, and blame shifting must be subdued and submitted to Christ, or it will sabotage the personal prophetic promise of great prosperity.*

7. *Misinterpretation and wrong application of personal prophecy will pervert God's purpose*

and stop the prophetic promise from ever coming to pass.

8. *The "Balaam motivation" of greed and gain, power and popularity, will hinder God's blessings on His prophetic promise to a person or project.*

Seeking Out the Prophet

The prophet can prophesy specific, revealing words concerning problems that are hindering a business, as well as new directions, activities, and goals. Many businessmen seek the prophet for confirmation before making major decisions in their endeavors. This is a scriptural practice. Most of the kings of Judah sought a word from a prophet to determine whether they should do certain things, such as going to war or building a building. They also inquired about whether certain endeavors would be profitable if they embarked upon them.

I was once ministering at a large church in Canada when the Lord revealed to me that there were many men in that service who owned their own businesses, but they were at a standstill. He told me there was a particular problem in each business that was the key hindrance. If I would give the invitation for them to come, He said, He would reveal each key problem.

Fifteen men who owned their own businesses came forward. They all knelt down in front of a row of chairs. I gave about two minutes of prophetic flow over each of them. To each one God spoke something different: To one He talked about problems in his accounting department; to another his need to cut back personnel and regroup and reevaluate; to another to expand into other fields.

The prophetic word told one man that God had been dealing with him for years about imbalance in his life between business and family, and that He was not going to bless his business anymore until he put things in proper order. His wife came to me the next day after her husband had taken some actions to obey the word of the Lord and said, "I have been telling my husband that for 20 years, but you did more in one night than I have been able to do in all these years!" The truth makes men free, and the prophetic anointing destroys the yoke of bondage (John 8:32; Isa. 10:27).

Present-day Example

A good example of how a prophet can help a businessman is given in Norvel Hayes's book *The Gift of Prophecy*. Hayes once attended a meeting where Kenneth Hagin was preaching in Cleveland, Tennessee. Prophet Hagin called him by name and gave him a personal prophecy about his finances. Many relevant truths can be derived from his personal testimony about what happened. Notice in the following excerpt how the personal prophecies gave warnings, instructions, consolation, hope of coming out on top again, additional prophecies through others for specific things to do, God's purpose for the process, and the end results for those who properly respond to personal prophecy and persevere until God's time for renewal of prosperity comes. Here is the personal prophecy from Kenneth Hagin, and how Norvel Hayes reacted:

> *The enemy is going to attack your finances, and a dark cloud will come upon your finances. But if you will keep working for Me, and be faithful, and if you will pray, and pray, and pray, and pray, and pray, you will come out of this attack. I will bring you out of the attack of the enemy, and you will be more financially successful than you have ever been.*

> *I said, Attack my finances? I don't have any financial problems...I own (along with the six restaurants) a manufacturing company, and I had my own sales distributing company. I was making from four to six thousand dollars a week, mostly from the distributing part of the business.*

> *About six months went by, and the sky fell on me. You talk about a dark cloud, it came upon me. All of a sudden, three of my restaurant managers turned flaky,*

and the restaurants were no longer making any money at all.

The following account is condensed from Norvel Hayes, *The Gift of Prophecy* (Tulsa, Oklahoma: Harrison House, 1980, page 20):

After that, Hayes discovered that one of his long-time secretaries had been stealing thousands of dollars from the manufacturing company. In less than one year he went from great prosperity to a battle for survival. Hayes remembered the word of Prophet Hagin, and kept praying and praying and praying. He resisted the temptation to pray with self-pity and unbelief, or to ask God, "Why me?" or bemoan his fate and become obsessed with trying to save the business to the exclusion of church and ministry. He made new dedications to God and resisted the devil by speaking his determination to do God's will and work regardless. He kept confessing God's word and decreeing to his checkbooks the abundance of finances.

How did God finally get him out? By more prophetic instructions. While visiting with his good minister friends, the Goodwins, sister Goodwin spoke a message in tongues to him and brother Goodwin gave the interpretation.

The prophetic message said: "If you will go to Tulsa, Oklahoma, for Me, I will show you two things after you get there." Norvel states that he only knew three people in Tulsa at that time, Roberts, Ford, and Hagin. He went to Kenneth Hagin's home. While there he prayed for Prophet Hagin's wife.

On the way to the airport, the prophet spoke to him and said, "Norvel, the Lord showed me that he sent you here for two reasons. First, to pray for my wife, and bring a blessing to her. And then, He told me to give you a prophecy."

*This was the prophecy Prophet Hagin gave him: "You have passed **My** test of faith. And because you have, son, you have obeyed Me. And because you have obeyed Me, My light is going to shine down from heaven. It is going to break through all the dark clouds, and shine upon you. It is going to shine upon your finances, and it shall come, and come, and come, in abundance to you."*

God began to bring some providential contacts, favor, and property sales, until in one day his bank account went from $85 to over $100,000. What is Norvel Hayes's conclusion about personally receiving a *rhema*, the operation of the gifts of the Holy Spirit, and prophets who give personal prophecies? Let him tell you in his own words:

Let me just pass this on to you. Prophecy, boiling up out of you supernaturally, will tell you where to go, and what to do, when you don't know where to go or what to do. I did not know that I was to call the Goodwins until the Lord spoke to me fifteen minutes before I was to leave on the plane to Chattanooga, Tennessee. I didn't know God wanted me to go to Tulsa until God spoke to me through the Goodwins. If I had not obeyed the word and gone to Tulsa I would not have been a special blessing to the Hagin household, nor would I have received the prophecy from the prophet that ended the three-year test and battle in the financial realm. When prophecy comes to you from God, through somebody that knows God, and you respect them, it can bring great blessings to you. Not only to you, but to many other people.

Notice some key prophetic principles here that are vital for faith to obey. When God tells someone to do something, He rarely tells them why, how, who, and when. Those details will be worked out later, after obedience is given to the first command. He said to Hayes, "Go to Tulsa and I will show you two things when you get there." It was like His word to Abraham, "Get out of thy country and go to the land that I will show thee." And like Abraham, Hayes "by faith...went out not knowing where he was going."

The preacher or businessman who insists on knowing more details before he will act in faith will never fulfill his prophetic promises for great success. If we can understand a word by human logic and can figure out how it can all work in detail, it is probably not a *rhema* from God, but rather our natural concepts. A divine word always takes divine faith to appropriate. Human reasoning and the five natural senses are normally the greatest hindrances to fulfilling personal prophecies.

Those who cannot take action based on God's Word alone should never go to a prophet for a word from the Lord. If they are going to do it their way and according to the world's standards for success, then they should not waste their time and the prophet's time by seeking a personal prophecy on their business and finances. *God's ways* and *carnal man's ways* are so different that when we try to mix the two, it confuses the whole situation (1 Cor. 2:14; Isa. 55:8-9).

This is the situation of most Christian businessmen who have dedicated their business to God but are still operating it according to the world's standards. If a person dedicates his business to God and asks God to bless, but will not do business according to God's directions, then he puts himself in the crosscurrents of self-destruction and bankruptcy. We must make up our minds and go all the way with one or the other to succeed.

The worldly man knows how to succeed financially and so does God. The principles and processes are similar, yet there is sufficient difference to make them incompatible. Both methods cannot be used in the same business and make it succeed, no more than gas and diesel can be put in the same tank and have the car run efficiently. Those who are dedicated and determined to operate their business upon God's Word, and are willing to act in faith, will greatly benefit from the ministry of the prophet and personal prophecy.

Why Some Businessmen and Women Do Not Succeed

Why can some Christians receive great prophecies about having great success and earning millions to give to the Church, yet never see it come to pass in their lifetimes? I know of three particular people, two men and one woman, who are a personification of this problem. I knew these people in a close ministry and business relationship for several years. They were charismatic Christians, and each in business for themselves. I prophesied to each of them more than once about their potential for great success and financial prosperity. Every prophet or saint who prophesied to them, and there were several who did, said the same things concerning their capabilities and calling.

Two of them, however, have never blessed the Kingdom of God financially. The woman was able to draw pastors, prophets, and national leaders in the Church and business world around her. She went from involvement in real estate, to gold mines, to oil, and world commodities. She was always on the verge of making millions, and she said she planned to give to the work of the Lord. Yet over the ten years I have known her, she has not blessed one person or church ministry with money. Instead she has ended up taking from everybody who has come close to her. My contact with her cost $2,000. Another prominent minister invested over $10,000 in her, with promises of millions, yet never received anything but hours of wasted time and dollars. Another prominent businessman, who was not a Christian, invested and lost over $100,000 for her to go to different nations, to get foreign capital at lower interest rates, and to arrange big oil and commodities deals.

The second person is a little different from the other two. He has a call to the ministry and is involved some in the Church. Every time you see him, he is on the verge of some great thing that will make millions for the Kingdom of God. He has about a dozen invention ideas, and numerous ministry ideas; but over the years not one of them has ever been productive.

I call the two people wolves in sheep's clothing who are being used by the devil to monopolize ministers' time and manipulate other Christians for their own purposes. They have visions of grandeur, but they are self-deceived and selfish. Their egotistical self-importance makes them really believe that they know everything and can do anything. They are spiritual leeches that draw their life and sustenance at the expense of others' lifeblood.

The third person is successful in his business, but it is at the expense of everyone who becomes involved with him. He not only has the "Jacob" spirit of manipulation and conniving, but he basically is not right in his motivation.

All three of these people in conversation and mannerism would make us think they are solely out for our success. They appear gregarious and unselfish. But every seemingly righteous act is performed with an ulterior motive for selfish personal gain. Every spiritual attribute is practiced for what it can profit them, and not because of a love for God and His ways.

Sadly enough, Christians are taught to be so loving, trusting, and helpful that they become gullible and easy prey for this type of "Christian." If the world were labeling these people, they would not try to be nice and explain that they have a "weakness" or are "immature." They would call them what they really are: con-artists.

People with wrong motivation and improper principles will never fulfill their personal prophecies, even if they were spoken by a mature, major prophet under the direct influence of the Holy Spirit. The soil of their soul is shallow and hard, and the deeper soil of their soul is filled with weed seeds of unrighteous practices. This type of people will never become productive and profitable to the Church until they allow God to break up their shallow ground and pull the weeds of unChristlikeness out of their lives. God has not allowed the prophets to expose these imposters in the Body of Christ yet. The tares and wheat are growing together until harvest time—but harvest time is nigh at hand. God hates false, selfish manipulation of His people for personal gain, whether it is in a Christian businessman, prophet, or pastor.

In conclusion, we should discuss the place of wisdom and balance in business and personal prophecy. We cannot run a business on personal prophecy from others, but we do need a word from the Lord occasionally to make it God's successful business. In my years of experience in this field, I have discovered that if we are called by God to be a businessman, then God gives the ability, wisdom, and knowledge needed to make it work. God's true calling includes the enablement for its accomplishment.

Though I am a prophet, very few of my decisions as president of Christian International School of Theology and CI Ministries are based on personal prophecies from others. I make the majority of my decisions on the "three W's" of God's Word, will, and way. Sometimes personal prophecy is instrumental in determining God's will and discovering God's way, but we must never become dependent upon prophecies from others to fulfill our mission in life.

If God has called a man to be a pastor, then God has given him the ability to prepare messages, counsel saints, and provide leadership to the flock. If the pastor has to call a prophet every week to ask him what he should preach on Sunday, then that man has become too dependent on the prophet, or else he has not been called to preach. If a businessman has to call the prophet or have some saint get him a word from the Lord before he can make daily administrative decisions, then he should not be in that position. People who are not gifted with creative administrative ability should be working somewhere else. A minister who cannot create new messages, preach with anointing, win souls, and mature God's people in ministry should move from the pulpit to the pew.

If we really believe God has called us to do what we are doing, then we should believe that His grace and wisdom is within us to do that work. But we must not become so self-sufficient that we refuse to call upon the prophet when he is needed, or listen to what he has to say if God sovereignly sends him to us with a word of instruction.

CHAPTER 11

PROPHETIC TERMINOLOGY

My wife has lived with me for over 32 years. She understands not only what I say, but also what I mean by most of my nonverbal communication through noises, gestures, and postures. She can usually grasp what I am trying to communicate even when she is not certain of the meaning of my particular words—not because she is an expert in linguistics, but because she is an expert in knowing Bill Hamon.

The same is true of our relationship to God. The longer we know Him and the more intimately acquainted we become with Him, the better we are able to understand His words to us and so respond to them appropriately. Understanding God's words to us is not as easy as it may seem at first. The Scriptures tell us that He thinks and expresses Himself according to a perspective that is much different from our own. God's ways, we are reminded, are as high above our ways as the heavens are high above the earth. So we must get to know God's prophetic terminology.

We believe that the Holy Spirit inspired and directed the writing of the Bible from the mind of God. So we should not be surprised to find that the Bible reveals to us something of the way God thinks. It shows us how He talks, and the human terms He uses to express Himself. In particular, we can look to the books of the prophets to find God's terminology, where there are so many quotes preceded by "thus saith the Lord."

We should remember as we read that a modern translation or paraphrase of Scripture will best help us gain a realistic understanding of how God would talk to someone in the twentieth century. Jesus did not speak in seventeenth-century King James English when He was here on earth, but rather in the common, everyday language of the people of His time. Jehovah declares Himself to be the "I AM," the ever-present-tense God who relates to every generation in their own language and customs. So if Jesus came personally to America to speak to Americans today, He would talk in their everyday language, using twentieth-century illustrations and modern terminology.

All that Jesus said demonstrated God's way of talking. By reading the Gospels as well as the prophets, and paying close attention to the words of Jesus there, we can gain a better understanding of the way God talks—which is what we will call prophetic terminology.

Prophetic Terminology of Time

Through both biblical study and personal experience, I have discovered that God's *time* terminology differs considerably from ours. Though He never seems to be in a hurry, He is always on time. But He often seems to take longer than we think He should.

Some of the greatest failures of the greatest figures of the Bible resulted from their impatience with God as they waited for a prophecy to be fulfilled. Abraham, for example, thought he was running out of time and tried to "help" God fulfill His word to him. The result was an Ishmael (Gen. 16). Whenever we jump ahead of God's timetable for prophetic fulfillment, we always produce something in the flesh that eventually opposes the fruit of the true prophetic promise.

Saul is another good example of this problem. He thought God had failed to come through on time as He had promised He would through the prophet Samuel. So Saul "forced" himself to disobey and offer the sacrifice instead of waiting for Samuel to arrive. That episode of impatience cost Saul his anointing, and cancelled God's prophetic word to him that his descendants would sit upon the throne of Israel (1 Sam. 13-18).

We may remember, too, how when Jesus heard that His friend Lazarus was critically ill, He waited four days before He went to him. The disciples thought Jesus went too late. When He arrived, Mary and Martha told Him that if He had come sooner, He could have done something, but there was no longer any hope because Lazarus was dead.

But Jesus always has the final verdict about whether or not it is too late. Today as then, even when it looks too late, Jesus can resurrect the dead. The marriage may be in the divorce court, the business may be heading for bankruptcy, the ministry opportunities may be gone, the doctors may give no hope, the hurricane may be coming right toward your home. But if God has spoken a clear prophetic promise to you, He will come through in time—His time. He will either be there in time to rescue the situation, or He will resurrect it to live again.

Knowing that God has His own time schedule can be an encouragement to those who are walking by faith while believing in God's faithfulness to bring forth His prophetic promise. But it can also be a frustration to the flesh, trying the patience of the saints. There was a time when nothing frustrated me more than to hear someone say, "Don't worry; it will happen in God's time" about something I wanted to happen right away. I resented and rejected that comment because I thought my faith would force God to work on my time schedule. No one, I reasoned, knew better than I did how desperately I needed and wanted it *now*. Tomorrow would simply be too late.

After more than 30 years, however, I have finally come to the realization that God does have a time and a season for things to happen. His schedule may not always make sense to the natural man's reasoning; our souls may cry out, "Why?" But I have learned, nevertheless, that His timetable is necessary for fullness, maturity, and bringing everything together in proper order. Consider just a few Scripture verses that make this evident:

*"When the **fullness of the time** was come, God sent forth His Son"* (Gal. 4:4a, emphasis added). *"Jesus Christ gave Himself a ransom for all, to be testified in **due time**"* (1 Tim. 2:6a, emphasis added). *"In **due time** Christ died for the ungodly"* (Rom. 5:6b, emphasis added). *"In the dispensation of the **fullness of times**, [God] might gather together in one all things in Christ"* (Eph. 1:10a, emphasis added). *"To every thing there is a **season**, and a **time** to every purpose under the heaven... a **time** for every work...everything beautiful in **His time**"* (Eccles. 3:1,11,17). *"It is not for you to know the **times** or the **seasons**, which the Father hath put in His own power. But ye shall receive power, after that the Holy Ghost is come"* (Acts 1:7-8a, emphasis added). *"Until the **time** that [Joseph's] word [of prophecy] came: the word of the Lord [tested] him"* (Ps. 105:19). *"Be not weary in well doing: for **in due season** we shall reap, if we faint not"* (Gal. 6:9, emphasis added).

God's Prophetic Terminology Concerning Certain Words

Suddenly or Immediately

When God uses the word *suddenly* or *immediately*, we need to understand them in the light of their biblical use. On the surface, it may seem that a sudden event has happened spontaneously. But if we look below the surface we find that a long time of preparation has led up to that sudden manifestation.

Acts 2:2, for example, tells us that *"**suddenly** there came a sound from heaven as of a rushing, mighty wind, and it filled all the house where they were sitting."* Because of the word *suddenly* we might tend to think that this was an unexpected surprise from God which no one had prepared for or believed for. But the truth is that 120 of Jesus' followers, including His apostles, had been faithfully praying, waiting, and believing for this supernatural visitation of the Holy Spirit—ever since

Jesus had told them to return to Jerusalem and wait for the promise of the Father (Acts 1:4-5).

"Suddenly" on the day of Pentecost they all began to speak with other tongues as they were baptized with the Holy Spirit. But this came about according to God's timetable, and man's preparation and placement. The apostles had received three and a half years of preparation, and had waited faithfully since Christ's ascension into Heaven. By the time the sun rose on the day of Pentecost, these faithful followers were right before God, their relationships were in order (they were "all in one accord"), they were at the right place, and God's fullness of time had come. So "suddenly" the promise of the Father was given, and they were endued with power from on high. When the day of Pentecost was *fully come*...then suddenly!

The word *immediately* was used by Jesus in a similar way. When He compared the establishment of the Kingdom of God to the planting of seed, He spoke of the "immediate" harvest at the end of the age (Mark 4:26-29). Yet the harvest only comes after the seed has been planted, has germinated while hidden in the earth, has sprouted a plant, and finally has produced a mature stalk of grain. When the grain is fully ripe, *then* "immediately" the farmer comes and harvests it. What is called "sudden" and "immediate," then, is actually based on progressive growth and preparation.

God plants within us a Kingdom seed, a vision, a divinely-inspired ministry or project. He causes it to grow without much notice by others, or even by ourselves. We keep praying and waiting, but nothing supernatural seems to be happening. It seems as though no one, not even God, will ever recognize, receive, and support the vision or ministry. But *suddenly*, when it has reached full maturity, when the person, the ministry, and God's purpose are ready, then *immediately* God harvests it by bringing it into full activity and fulfillment. It is then mightily manifested to the Church and the world.

Consequently, we should not worry about when God will move to fulfill the vision and manifest the ministry He has given us. Our job is to keep watering the seed and weeding the soil. We must simply keep doing what we have to do, believing in the ministry, confessing its fulfillment, and moving in the direction of the harvest. Only the Master Husbandman knows the proper time, and when things are done in His ordained time, our ministry will be firmly maintained, our lives preserved, Christ glorified, the saints edified, and the world reconciled to God.

Now or *This Day*

When we hear the words *now* or *this day* we usually think "immediately" or "within 24 hours." In prophetic terminology, however, these terms do not always have their everyday meaning.

In the first two years of King Saul's reign, he received a personal prophecy from the prophet Samuel. Saul had failed to obey a previous word from the Lord, and so Samuel prophesied judgment upon him by telling him that *now* his kingdom would not continue. If we had heard that prophecy, we probably would have expected it to come to pass immediately. But in God's prophetic timetable, *now* was 38 years later. It was not until then that Saul lost his kingdom (1 Sam. 13:1-14).

A few years later, Samuel gave Saul another personal prophecy with specific instructions about what he should do. But Saul did not obey the word in detail. So the prophet Samuel had to give him another word of judgment: *"The Lord hath rent the kingdom of Israel from thee **this day**, and hath given it to a neighbor of thine, that is better than thou"* (1 Sam. 15:28, emphasis added). Once again, God's prophetic term did not mean what we might assume it meant; *this day* did not mean that Saul's reign would end within 24 hours. It was some 24 years later that the kingdom was transferred to David.

A valuable insight into God's personal prophetic process is provided by this story of Saul and Samuel. When personal prophecy comes forth, it is divinely decreed and established in the spiritual, heavenly realm. But it may be many years before it is fulfilled in the natural realm. For that reason, we must not judge a prophecy false simply because it did not come to pass in the time we had assumed.

If a prophecy spells out an exact time and date—"Thus saith the Lord, 'You will receive a check for $50,000 by noon on July 29, 1989' " —then we can declare that portion of it false if it does not come to pass at the specific time given. But if it uses phrases like "very soon," "this day," "now," or "in the near future," we should not put any time limits on the prophetic word.

The Bible says that God talks about things that are not now as though they are: Abraham *"believed...God, who...calleth those things **which are not** as **though they were**"* (Rom. 4:17, emphasis added). Because of this principle of prophetic terminology, it is sometimes difficult to determine whether a personal prophecy is speaking of things past, present, or future.

Based on biblical examples and my own years of experience, however, I have found the following timetable for prophetic terminology to be helpful, but not rigid:

> **Immediately** means from one day to three years.
> **Very soon** means one to ten years.
> **Now** or **this day** means one to forty years.
> **I will** without a definite time designation means God will act sometime in the person's life if he is obedient.
> **Soon** was the term Jesus used to describe the time of His soon return almost two thousand years ago. *"Behold, I come quickly."*

Prophetic Terms Implying Particular Processes

Certain prophetic terms imply that corresponding processes will accompany them to bring about their fulfillment. God's character traits, the fruits of the Holy Spirit, are divine seeds planted in the soil of the redeemed soul which must be cultivated. So He prepares the ground of our life situations to work certain graces into our lives, such as patience, wisdom, love, and faith. If God speaks prophetically that He plans to give us some of these traits, or that we will manifest them mightily, we must understand the corresponding processes we will be taken through to grow them.

We tend not to live by supernatural supply unless our human resources become insufficient. So God must arrange our circumstances to force us to receive His divine graces in order to survive. The following words in a prophecy should alert us that God will be working in the corresponding ways to bring it to pass in our lives:

Patience

When a personal prophecy promises that we will have great patience, we must remember the words of Romans 5:3 that *tribulation* is the soil in which patience grows. Problems, pressures, trials, and time delays force us to allow the Holy Spirit to work divine enablement through these times of heart-breaking, mind-blowing, world-shaking situations, giving us experiences of overcoming that increase our hope. And hope makes us not ashamed to believe again, for the love of God, which is patience personified, is shed abroad in our hearts by the Holy Spirit.

Wisdom

When God says prophetically that He will give us wisdom, that means He will allow some problems and situations to arise that are beyond our capacity to solve. They will thus force us to draw on God's wisdom, giving Him an opportunity to fulfill His promise. After all, we really have no need of divine wisdom unless all sources of human wisdom have been exhausted and proven insufficient to solve a problem.

Love

When a prophetic word tells us that we will manifest God's divine love, it means that we will be dealing with some unlovable people. They will do things that will destroy all our human love, so that the only way we can love them is to draw on God's *agape*, which can love even the most unlovable. Normally, it will be someone near and dear to us. Instead of resisting and resenting, we must repent and receive God's love for the person.

Faith

We can have three kinds of faith: saving faith, the gift of faith, and the Spirit's fruit of faith. When we are told in prophecy that we will have great faith, we should realize that the soil of the fruit of faith is life on the brink of disaster in need of a miracle. If we never are put in a position by God where we cannot meet our own needs by our own means, then we will never grow the fruit of faith.

Build, Expand, Increase

Sometimes God says, "I am going to build, increase, expand." But to build more, a deeper foundation must be laid for a greater building. And that means we must first tear down the old building, dig up the old, limited foundation, and lay a new one for a ten-story ministry instead of a one-story ministry. These terms therefore imply some uprooting of ministry and some soul-stretching experiences.

Great Harvest

When God declares by personal prophecy that He will give us a great harvest, then the prophetic process will move according to the stage we are in when we receive the word. If a farmer were to receive such a prophecy, he would probably know from practical experience what to expect.

Take, for example, a corn farmer in the midwestern United States. If he received this prophetic word in August after he had plowed his corn for the last time, he would know there was nothing for him to do but trust that God would give sufficient rain to bring the corn on to maturity and protect it from storms so he could reap at the proper time. If he received that prophetic word in January, however, he would know there was much he would have to do to cooperate with the prophecy so it would come to pass. He would have to break up the fallow ground, prepare the soil for planting the seed in straight rows, sow the seed, cultivate the soil, fertilize, water regularly, and spray against diseases and insects. Then he would have to harvest immediately when the crop was mature.

A prophetic word about a spiritual harvest requires the same dedication, diligence, cooperation, and response. Faith without works is dead, and confession is not possession. Simply proclaiming our prophecy will not fulfill the promise without obedience as well.

If we truly believe God's personal prophetic promise to us concerning a great ministry, then, like the farmer, we must start now to cooperate with the word so we will be ready for its fulfillment in due season. By faith we must begin our preparation, practicing patiently until the promise is procured. If we do not have faith to prepare ourselves even when no ministerial opportunity is in sight, or when we fail to see how it can become a reality, we will miss our opportunity to participate in the promise.

Biblical Examples

Noah's obedience would have been too late if he had waited to build the ark until he saw rain. David had to be faithful tending sheep, killing the lion and the bear, before he could face the giant. The three kings of Israel, Judah, and Edom had to have the ditches dug in the desert before Elisha's prophetic promise of water would come to pass. Sometimes the preparation process will not make any sense to our natural reasoning. But if we prepare anyway, God will provide abundantly according to His prophetic word.

Great Victory

If we hear that a great victory is coming, but we are not currently fighting a battle, then we need to be prepared for one. We cannot have a great victory without a great battle; little battles bring only little victories. So whenever we hear words like *victorious*, *overcomer*, or *more than a conqueror*, we can be assured of a fight. But we can also be confident of victory.

Restoration

The word *restoration* has two meanings. When God says He will restore certain *things* to us, that means we will regain what we have lost. But if He says He will restore *us*, then He is talking about the kind of process that goes on when an old automobile is restored. We will be taken completely apart piece by piece, scattered over the garage, sandblasted to remove rust spots, given new parts to replace those that are worn out, and then reassembled and repainted. We will first become a greater mess of confusion and debris before we are restored.

New Revelation, Vision, Bring Forth a Ministry

This is the kind of terminology the angel Gabriel used when he gave Mary her personal prophecy about bringing forth a ministry (Christ) that would bless the world. The natural process she had to endure to bear Jesus is parallel to the spiritual process we must undergo to bring forth a divinely ordained ministry.

Before there can be a birthing process, we must have a close relationship with God that gives opportunity for the Holy Spirit to plant a seed of faith and vision. The vision then grows like a baby in the womb of our spirit. Patience, adjustments, and divine flexibility are required for the long process from conception to delivery.

Like an expectant mother's womb, our soul is stretched until we feel we cannot stretch anymore. We become as awkward in our spiritual walk, feeling out of shape, as a pregnant woman does physically, especially in the last month of pregnancy. And even though, like the pregnant woman, we feel after "nine months" that we have had all we can endure, like her we find out that things get worse before they get better. The hardest labor pains come at delivery.

Just before a vision, ministry, or prophetic promise is brought forth into visible reality, we go through our darkest hour of labor and stress. Like many women in childbirth we begin to think *Why did I ask for this? I don't want to go through with this—it's not worth it!* But if we hold on, flowing and working with the labor pains instead of against them, before we know it, the results of our labor will be full and rewarding. We will have a ministry come forth for all to see.

Like a new baby, that ministry will go through several years when we must take care of it day and night. It will be wholly dependent on us. But as we pour our life, energy, time, and ability into it, just like a child it will eventually take care of itself. All it will need is our parental vision, care, counsel, and covering.

Worldwide Ministry, Recognition, Success, Millionaire Ministry

Most people who have the potential for great prosperity and powerful performance fail to produce. Even some Spirit-filled Christians who have received numerous prophecies about their great potential and God's purpose for their lives never see these prophecies come to pass. Why not? Because they are not willing to pay the price—to go through the divine process required—for obtaining the promise.

The mightier the ministry, the more time God takes to make the man or woman. The greater the prophetic promise of powerful performance, the longer the process of preparation. Personal prophecies about great exaltation and worldwide recognition mean that we will first face humbling experiences of seeming failure, rejection, and abandonment, feelings of being a nobody going nowhere doing nothing. This was true of God's preparation for David, Joseph, Abraham, and Moses.

Those who suddenly become "successful" without going through the proper process will usually not be able to maintain their personal purity or go on to maturity and the fullest possible ministry. They may keep their position, but they will lose God's presence, as well as their priorities and their dedication to the divine purpose. King Saul and Solomon are two good examples of this kind of tragedy.

For this reason, we should deeply appreciate God's preparation for possessing prophetic promises. With the proper attitude and understanding of what is taking place, we can actually take pleasure and encouragement in the process, even when it is not in itself pleasant. That is why Paul could say, *"I glory in my infirmities, that the power of Christ may rest upon me"* (2 Cor. 12:9b; see also 12:10).

If we are not willing to go through the necessary process, we should not believe and pray for the fulfillment of personal prophecies about great power, position, or prosperity. If we are not willing for God to mold and make us for a mighty ministry, we should not expect it. It is better to stay small and maintain our present ministry than to become a "Saul" and lose it all.

I Will, You Will, We Will

When God says "I will" about great things *He* plans to do, He does not mean that He will act by Himself apart from our involvement and participation. When He says, "I will," He means, "we will"; "I will do it in you and through you, I will enable you to do it."

God said "I will" to Moses seven times concerning Egypt, the children of Israel, and Canaan. He begins with: *"...I will bring you out from under the burdens of the Egyptians...And I will bring you in unto the land"*...and ends with...*"I will give it you for an heritage: I am the Lord!"* (Exod. 6:6-8) There is no explicit mention here of any responsibility on the part of Israel. It sounds like an unconditional, absolute prophecy that is not dependent upon the human element at all, but relies instead on the divine purpose.

As we know from the Exodus story, however, God's "I will" meant that He would cooperate with their own efforts: "I will work supernaturally in those areas where you cannot work naturally. I will deal with the other parties involved and take care of the other end of the situation. I will be the hidden, invisible, powerful force enabling you to perform victoriously. I will give you miracles to manifest, wisdom to walk in My ways and work My will, and patience to prevail until you obtain the prophetic promise."

On the other hand, when God says, "You will," He also means "we will." Take Gideon, for example. When the angel of the Lord gave him his personal prophecy, he said, *"The Lord is with you, you mighty man of valor...You go in this your might and you shall save Israel from the hand of the Midianites: have I not sent you?"* (Judg. 6:12-14)

No wonder Gideon needed some assurances before he would go! The whole emphasis seemed to be on him and his own resources. And the further he progressed in the endeavor, the more ridiculous it all became when viewed in the natural. When it came time to fight, he had only three hundred men, some jugs, and some lamps. But God fought with him, and he prevailed.

Whether the prophetic terminology is "I will" or "you will," God always means *"We* will." We will be the mortal presence on earth performing, and He will be the invisible force in the heavens working miracles.

Understanding all these prophetic terms are critical for faith and patience to cooperate with the prophetic process until it has its perfect result.

CHAPTER 12

PROPHECIES RELATING TO PREGNANCIES, BIRTHS, AND BABIES

All the prophets I have known over the years have had experiences where God led them to give a word of prophecy to women concerning becoming pregnant and giving birth. Some have even prophesied whether it would be a boy or girl. Most of the time the couples receiving these prophecies have not been able to have children up to this time. I have personally given prophecies to scores of married couples over the years who were not able to have children, yet nine months later a child would be born. For some it was a medical impossibility to conceive and give birth at the time the prophetic word came forth.

Prophecies that produce miracles for the barren are not given at the discretion and will of man. But prophets and prophetesses must speak as they are moved by the Holy Spirit. At the same time, there are a few biblical examples where the man of God spoke, seemingly without being sovereignly directed, yet still the miracle was wrought. Elisha, for example, wanted to show appreciation to the couple who had built him a prophet's chamber in their home. He suggested several things he could do for her such as mentioning her to the king, but she did not want any of the things he suggested. When Elisha asked Gehazi his servant if he had any ideas, he mentioned that the woman was married to a man much older than herself, and that they had no children. Perhaps, he suggested, that would be a way to bless her for her kindness to the prophet.

Elisha called the woman to him and said to her, *"About this season, according to the time of life, thou shalt embrace a son."* Approximately nine months later she had a son. In this case there is no scriptural indication that God told Elisha to prophesy to her that she would have a son. He seems simply to have pulled upon his mature prophet anointing and faith to speak a creative word to her (2 Kings 4:8-18).

Another example is Hannah. She lived several years as a barren wife to her husband, Elkanah. Hannah prayed and interceded for years to have a baby, and one day she was at the altar in the temple in travail before the Lord. Eli, the senior priest, was so spiritually dull and insensitive that he did not discern her heart, but rather assumed from her actions that she was drunk. Hannah explained to him that she was not drunk, but was in deep grief and travail for God to give her a son. Eli responded by saying, *"Go in peace: and the God of Israel grant thee thy petition that thou hast asked of Him."* There is no indication in Scripture that Eli said this by divine inspiration; he seems to have spoken simply from the authority of his office of priest and prophet. Happily, Hannah did not let the man of God's false accusation against her, his lack of spiritual perception or divine inspiration, hinder her from laying hold of the word she was believing for. He stood as God's only representative in that day and hour, so she took it as a word from the Lord. She went home with her husband and conceived and bore a son, Samuel, the prophet (1 Sam. 1:1-20).

Numerous women in the Bible were prophetically told they would conceive before it happened. Some were even told what sex the baby would be and what his name should be. Manoah and his wife were told ahead of time; Zacharias and Elizabeth and Mary were even told what to name their babies and what their ministries would be. Isaiah and Hosea the prophets were told the names to give their children, because their names would be a living prophecy to the nation of Israel. God told Abraham and Sarah ahead of time that they would have a son and what they should name him. There are more than enough examples in the Bible to show that God does reveal information to some couples ahead of time about the conception and birth of babies.

Some Present-day Examples

In my personal prophetic ministry, I have heard about a hundred testimonies of conception and birth that took place after personal prophecy to the couple or just the wife. A few of these are useful for illustrating some vital principles about rhema and personal prophecy in this area. The prophecies that produced supernatural miracles of healing so that conception could occur, and the pregnancy brought to proper birthing, are factual realities. These prophecy testimonies of married couples are clear evidence that miracles can take place through prophecy enabling them to conceive and give birth to their own child.

Prophetic Miracles

I was once prophesying over a church group at a family camp in Prescott, Arizona. A couple was there with a singing group from Utah. I prophesied over them that God was giving them the desires of their heart and answering their prayers for children. Nine months later a child was born to them. They testified later that they had been trying for seven years to have children and were unable to do so. When I visited their church some time later the grandmother of the young mother told me how she had interceded for her granddaughter to have children for seven years. The whole church had been praying as well, because they were prominent in leadership and known by everyone.

From this event we can observe that personal prophecy miracles are like the miracle of a soul getting saved in that they are often the end result of many prayers for a person or situation. Personal prophecy is a tool of God to answer our prayers, in which He finds a voice to speak His creative miracle into existence and fulfillment. Sometimes personal prophecy is a seed-sowing ministry to bring the first thought and faith for certain things; other times it is a watering and cultivating ministry to bring encouragement and direction for the person to press on to harvest time. At still other times it is a harvest time ministry, speaking the consummating words that finalize the process and bring immediate manifestation and fulfillment of a promise.

Unexpected Prophecies of Birth

Sometimes God prophetically decrees things that a couple has not been particularly desiring or praying for. Just a couple of examples can demonstrate this point.

One man wrote a long testimony of many things that had come to pass through the prophecies I had spoken to him, including the birth of their little girl.

My wife and I had been married only about a year, and neither of us had ever conceived the idea of having a child of our own since my wife had been a widow with two children for several years. I was 47 and she was 40 when we got married.

We had kept some foster children and had discussed keeping others, so when you prophesied that we would have an addition to our family and a financial blessing, we just assumed that it meant we would take in some foster kids and be paid for keeping them. But about 14 months later that prophecy was fulfilled when my wife became pregnant and eventually gave birth to a baby girl, whom we named Mary Joann.

The doctor suggested we consider abortion because of my wife's age. I told him, "No! The God that spoke this new addition to our family will cause this baby to be born

*healthy and normal"—and praise God, He did. Mary
Joann is now a healthy and beautiful six-year-old.*

Preventing Frustration

We recently had a situation on our staff in which the couple was not ready for another addition to their family. But the prophet spoke, and things happened. Scott and Kathy Webster have been with CI for five years. At the January '86 CI Prophets seminar, one of our network of prophets spoke to them and said, "You are going to have your first son in January, 1987." They were excited about the promise of having a boy, but not the date of arrival. Their oldest daughter, Johanna, was only two years old, and their second daughter, Bethany, was only six months old. Kathy definitely did not want another baby in twelve months, which would give her three children age three and under.

God did not have the prophet speak this word to bring about a creative miracle for conception, for Kathy had no problems with becoming pregnant. It was not an answer to years of praying and longing to have a child. Though it did fulfill a father's desire to have a son, this desire was not an obsession with Scott. So why did God reveal it, and why did the prophet speak it forth?

I believe it was primarily to let Kathy know that it was God's will for them to have their first son in 1987. The word helped her avoid being frustrated at becoming pregnant so soon again. It brought confirmation ahead of time that this conception was not a careless accident, but rather had come about in God's timing and purpose for their lives.

The couple took preventive measures to keep pregnancy from occurring, hoping the prophet was seeing a "nine" instead of a "seven," and that they would have their first son in 1989. But the word came to pass anyway. Steven Scott Webster was born January 22, 1987.

Giving Hope to Hang On and Keep Believing

Sometimes God gives a *rhema* or has the prophet speak a personal prophecy about having a baby in order to keep hope alive until God's work is accomplished and His proper timing fulfilled for pregnancy. Our daughter and son-in-law waited two years before trying to start their family. Sherilyn was not able to become pregnant during the following three years.

Glenn helped minister at the CI Prophets conferences and also had numerous prophets speak at his church, so Sherilyn received numerous prophecies during those years. She was ministered to by ten or twelve prophets, plus other saints, who gave her *rhemas* about her having babies. Some would prophesy a boy and some a girl. One prophesied a boy and a girl. She wondered if she would have twins! At one seminar a prophet prophesied she was going to have a son, and a pastor gave a word of knowledge that she was going to have a daughter. Their terminology would have made one think she was pregnant right then, but two years later she was still not pregnant.

Sherilyn was raised in a prophet's home and had flowed in prophecy since her teenage years. But she grew discouraged. She said to me, "Daddy, I am so tired of hearing prophecies about becoming pregnant. I don't want to hear another prophecy about having children; I want to get pregnant!"

I had given a prophecy to their church for them to build a big nursery, for God was going to start sending in young couples and cause all the marriageable singles in their church to get married and have children. At that time there was only one couple in the church with nursery-age children. Two years later they had over 15 in the nursery. Children were being born all around her. Her two older brothers had produced two daughters each, and she had produced none. She felt like Hannah, thinking, *What's the matter with me? Why can't I produce?*

Finally God gave her a time schedule. A pastor-prophet from Kentucky attended the January '85 CI Prophets seminar, and stopped at Glenn and Sherilyn's house to visit. While there he felt the Lord gave him a word concerning her becoming pregnant, but because he had heard me talk at the seminar about Sherilyn receiving so many words about this, and how frustrating it had become to her, he did not give her the word. Even so, the word would not go away when he arrived back home. So he finally wrote her a short note: "Sherilyn, I felt the Lord spoke to me that you will have your first baby by December of this year. Since this is the month of February, I guess it won't take long to find out whether this is a true word or just my imagination." Sure enough, Sherilyn gave birth to Charity Faith on November 15, 1985. The prophetic word came to pass.

On February 5, 1987, Sherilyn gave birth to Joshua Glenn Miller. She then said, "Mom, you can quit praying so hard; it's working now."

Which prophet was right? The one who prophesied a boy or the one who prophesied a girl, or the one who prophesied a boy and a girl? All of them were right. She had a girl and a boy within 15 months. Sherilyn's experience should teach us not to try to figure out how, what, and when; we should just believe and be encouraged to press on in faith, until the time comes for His word to be fulfilled in our life.

Extra Assurance Given Because of Greater Miracle and Longer Process

Why does God give so many prophecies to some and hardly any to others, even when they both spend the same amount of time around the prophets? Many prophecies are given because it will take more than the laws of nature to bring them to pass. Greater than normal faith, patience, and perseverance will be required. So numerous prophecies saying the same thing are given by God to encourage those who are easily discouraged, and to bring reassurance that something really is the will of God, and will eventually come to pass according to God's timing and purpose.

Sometimes prophecies about babies involve a multitude of things that must be accomplished in several different areas before it is according to God's wisdom and timing for that word to come to pass. If God is using barrenness to accomplish certain things in the lives of the married couple, then He will not let their desire and the prophetic word about babies come to pass until that work has been accomplished. The following detailed testimony of one family is typical of this reality.

The husband of this couple is an attorney and the wife is a registered nurse. We had a CI extension college at Trinity Temple, West Palm Beach, Florida, where they attended. I was there several times for the college and for spiritual meetings during a three-year period from their first personal prophecy until its fulfillment. I prophesied to them each time, and each time the prophecy included something about having children. Since they had not yet conceived, this one time they asked for counsel. So we spent most of an afternoon going over all their prophecies and discussing whether or not the prophetic word implied they would become natural parents. After close evaluation and counsel, we concluded that the word said they were going to "have" children, which did not specify that she had to conceive and give birth. Therefore, they could go ahead with adoption proceedings.

The next time I prophesied to them, however, the prophecy used the words *conceive* and *give birth*. That wiped out our four hours of counsel with great conclusions about adoption! Both the written words and the unspoken realities of this couple's testimony are important because many principles of God's process for prophetic fulfillment are revealed in this mother's testimony. Like Hannah's case in the Bible, this situation shows that delays are not denials, but are designed to bring dedication:

> *My husband and I had been trying several years to have children when you gave us our first prophecy concerning this matter in September, 1977. All symptoms indicated it would take a miracle for this to happen. Our fertility tests were not encouraging. Specifically, I had severe*

endometriosis (scar tissue in the pelvis) which was becoming increasingly spread over my reproductive organs; frequent large ovarian cysts which ruptured and threatened me with surgery; and cervical mucus hostility which prevented all or most sperm from surviving more than a very few hours. Richard's sperm count was low-normal, which didn't help matters. My doctor had sent me to specialists, who were unable to define any treatments which could help with any hope of success, though we tried every available treatment short of surgery—which had no guarantees, either.

The first two times you prophesied to us, the prophetic word spoke of us having children, of a need of a creative miracle in my body to fulfill my cry for fruitfulness. The third time you came, we asked for counsel before you had a chance to prophesy to us again. I was becoming so frustrated and confused and emotional about having children. I wanted it so bad, and God had spoken through His prophet that it was His will, but nothing was happening. After several hours of counseling we all mutually agreed that we should go ahead with the adoption process, in case that was God's plan for us.

During these years, I took medication which was new on the market for endometriosis, which we felt was part of God's plan for my healing, and which helped my condition somewhat. Then three months after I had stopped taking the medication, my endometriosis became quite worse again, and my doctor seriously considered surgery. We reminded my doctor that we believed God would heal me so that I could have the children He had promised us. Then I went home and cast myself totally on the mercy of God for the completion of my healing, knowing that I must be healed before I could conceive.

Dr. Bill, you returned to Trinity Temple in West Palm Beach, Florida, again in October, 1979. After you finished preaching, about 9:00 p.m., you prophesied over people till after midnight. We were one of the last couples you prophesied over.

You gave us a long prophecy which covered many areas of our life, and again the word about children came forth. This time it was much more specific, answering some particular questions we had and clearing up some confusion and indecisions. I had asked God to take away the desire for a child of my own flesh if He intended to give us an adopted child, but I became more desirous than ever to conceive. Nothing had happened with our adoption application, not even an interview.

I will not try to put in words the mental and emotional battles I was having. As Dr. Bill prophesied, several words of instruction and encouragement came, such as "The timing is in God's hands...Reap in due time... Enter into rest and peace...Cease frustrating yourself... Does not a Father want to be a grandfather to His daughter?...For with joy shall you bring forth, saith the Lord...with joy shall you conceive."

That certainly answered any questions in our minds about adoption! The reminder of the Lord that the timing of things was in His hands kept us going on in our walk of faith as God completed my physical healing and began to work on some spiritual matters.

In March of 1980, we attended a Jesus '80 conference in Orlando, and God put His finger on so many areas of my life that He was not satisfied with. He made it clear that, regardless of what others with children did or said, I was not to consider them, but I must consider what God required of me. He made it painfully clear to me that until I got down to business with Him in these areas He had pointed out, He would **not** *allow us to have children. So I got to work!*

When you came back again in May of 1980, you prophesied over us again, and again it was after midnight. But this time there were words of great assurance and confirmation of what had been transpiring in my life. The personal prophecy confirmed the stretching and maturing process that I had been going through, so that I was now ready with a motherhood ability, knowledge, and understanding. God spoke to me through His prophet: "I would not do it until your faith matured, until your trust matured, until your understanding matured, because that was more important to Me than your continual calling out to Me about the matter of motherhood." Oh, what peace and rest came to my soul!

Praise God! Two months after that prophecy, in July of 1980, God performed His miracle of healing which enabled conception to take place. In May of 1981, our precious little girl was born. My pregnancy, labor, and delivery were models of God's perfection, even to His sparing me of morning sickness so that I could continue to run my business. Once the prophetic breakthrough comes, God does exceedingly abundantly above all we can ask or think.

Later I conceived again and God gave us a beautiful son. Our daughter is now in kindergarten and our son is healthy and growing.

Thank God for prophets and personal prophecy. If it had not been for the personal prophecy assuring us that God wanted us to have children and then instructing us that we would have our own, we probably would not have had the knowledge and faith to keep going until God worked the miracle. We might have been pressured into having the operation and gone for years trying to adopt. I do not know what all we would have done without the prophet and personal prophecy but I do know what we have been able to do with the blessings of the prophet and personal prophecy ministry.

This couple believed in God and were established. They believed God's prophet and prospered. They received a prophet in the name of a prophet and received the prophet's reward.

The greatest reward of believing and receiving a prophet is that it causes the words he gives you to come to pass. To reject the word of the prophet is to reject the prophet; to reject a God-sent prophet is to reject God. So we must be sure to follow the principles of a proper response to personal prophecy in order to derive the maximum benefits.

A Long Process of Transformation

Another woman, from Indianapolis, had a similar long, drawn-out process, followed by a miracle through the prophecy of prayer by the prophet. In her 12 years of marriage without children she suffered from an extreme case of hypoglycemia, causing side effects of schizophrenia; emergency surgery from a burst tumor; a partial hysterectomy; and endometriosis surrounding all the reproductive organs. When she was born again in 1976, the hypoglycemia, infections, and schizophrenia left immediately. Three years later, doctors found a large growth covering the opening of her uterus, indicating cancer. This is her testimony concerning the prophetic ministry to her:

On January 8, 1982, you were ministering in the afternoon. You had just prophetically ministered the gift of healing to a woman. You wanted to activate that gift by having someone come forward who needed healing so that you and the lady would pray for them. I came forth.

You asked what my problem was, and I just said "pain." You immediately said, "It's female problems." Then you both laid hands on me and prayed for a creative miracle.

A couple of months later, when I went to a Christian doctor, he confirmed that I was pregnant, calculating my due date from the time you prayed for me. He also confirmed that there was no cancer, nor any growth over the uterus. He said I had a very clear uterus and was in excellent health. He was somewhat surprised that I was nearing 40!

Our daughter was born nine months and three days after you prayed for me. For reasons I don't understand, though perhaps because some fear of doctors needed to be eliminated, I had to have her by cesarean section. Through this surgery it was confirmed that there was no endometriosis around any of my organs.

My doctor's partner, a Jewish man, was the one who did the cesarean section. He had an opportunity to witness all this before surgery, and then it was confirmed by my medical chart.

Having this child has worked something in me as a woman and has given me a fulfillment that is hard to put into words. This truly has been a miracle, and we rejoice in our little girl, giving praise and glory to our Lord Jesus Christ.

Would this woman have had all of these miracles if she had not come to know God, and become exposed to the gifts of the Holy Spirit and the ministry of the prophet? We cannot say for sure, but I believe the chances are very slim. We do know what did happen to her when she was saved and later received the ministry of the prophet.

If you are in need of a miracle, if your heart is crying out to know what God's purpose and timing is for your life, then you need to find a place where gifts of the Holy Spirit are being manifested and prophets are prophesying. Do not limit yourself to some immature and "spooky spiritual" Christian giving you some strange words. Go to a mature pastor for counsel and find a mature, anointed prophet for a prophetic word of instruction and a creative miracle of healing. If you have been discouraged and disillusioned by the immature, ignorant, presumptuous, or counterfeit gifts and prophets, do not give up. There are true gifts of the Holy Spirit being manifested, and there are true, upright, compassionate, and God-anointed prophets in the land today. God has a remedy for your situation. Renew your hope. Seek God and get among the company of prophets God is raising up in this generation. Make yourself available for God to speak to you through His prophets and to work a miracle in your behalf.

Chapter 13

The Nature of Personal Prophecy

In order to respond properly to God's Word for us, we must first recognize three characteristics that are true of all personal prophecies. However it may be worded, a personal prophecy will always be *partial, progressive*, and *conditional.* Each of these qualities must be understood to fulfill God's word in our lives.

We Prophesy in Part

First, we must remember Paul's statement to the Corinthians: *"For we know in part, and we prophesy in part"* (1 Cor. 13:9). Just as a word of knowledge is only a fragment of God's infinite knowledge, a prophecy is only a small insight into God's will for our lives.

We are told in Deuteronomy 29:29 that *"the secret things belong unto the Lord our God: but those things which are revealed belong unto us and our children for ever, that we may do all the words of this law."* God only reveals what we need to know in order to do His will more perfectly at that particular time and place. Those things He does not want us to know at the time He keeps secret from the one prophesying. Prophet Elisha said, *"The Lord hath hid it from me"* (2 Kings 4:27b).

A good illustration of the incomplete nature of prophecy is the biblical promise of the Messiah. Each of the Messianic prophecies only provides one small piece of the picture puzzle that told of Jesus' coming: David was promised an eternal Heir for his throne, Isaiah was told of a Suffering Servant, Daniel saw the victorious coming of the Son of Man. No one prophecy told it all.

The same is true of our personal prophecies. A word from God will only cover a portion of God's will for us—perhaps with regard to a single "chapter" of our life story, or a particular area of activity. Sometimes God will speak about our ultimate ministry, but will not tell us about the process of trials and other ministries we will have in the meantime.

This was the case with Joseph. His prophetic dreams revealed that he would rule over his brothers, but did not include any mention of his being sold into slavery, his problems with Potiphar's wife, or his time in prison. A number of years passed before Joseph was able to see the whole picture of God's plan for his life. The same was true for Abraham, David, and many others.

Understanding that prophecy always reveals only a part of God's word to us keeps us from despairing when a prophecy fails to mention a specific area of concern. Just because God says nothing just now about a particular ministry, for example, does not mean that such a ministry will never be.

At the same time, knowing the incomplete nature of prophecy should keep us from presuming that God's silence about a particular matter implies His approval. If we have hidden in our lives a certain problem, bondage, or disobedience, yet the prophecy we receive speaks positively about our lives, we cannot conclude that God condones our sin. Perhaps the best example of this principle can be seen in the life of Moses.

Moses received directly from God several words of personal prophecy concerning his great call to deliver three million people from bondage and take them into Canaan. After demonstrations that God would work miracles in his behalf, he was finally willing to go, and began his journey back to Egypt. Yet on the way, God met him at an inn and *sought to kill him* for a particular matter of disobedience: He failed to circumcise his sons according to the Abrahamic covenant (Exod. 4:24-26).

The long prophecy God had given Moses previously about his great ministry had not revealed this area of sin in his life. But the silence certainly did not mean that God approved of it. I have seen the same situation many times with Christians and even ministers. Over a period of years they receive many positive prophecies from prophets and prophetic presbyteries, yet all along they have had serious sin in their life. The long-suffering and mercy of God prevented the sin from coming to light as long as the person was willing and honestly desiring to be delivered from it.

On the other hand, some of those same people eventually concluded that because their ministry was functioning successfully, and no prophetic mention was made of their sin, God must not be concerned about it. But the moment the person began justifying him or herself that way, God began setting in motion events that would shout from the housetops what had been going on in secret.

Prophecy Unfolds Progressively

The second characteristic of personal prophecy is that it is *progressive*. It unfolds and expands gradually over the years, with each prophetic word adding new information and revelation. As the details of God's will and way accumulate, He slowly unveils His full plan for our lives and His means for bringing them to pass.

The life of Abraham is a beautiful portrayal of this reality. His *first* word from the Lord, when he was about 50 years old, simply told him to leave his country and go to a land the Lord would show him (Acts 7:3). He obeyed and went to Haran with his family, but he knew nothing more about what God had in mind.

The *second* prophecy came to Abraham when he was 75, this time with more explicit instructions. The first word was reemphasized, and he was told to leave Haran and keep moving. God also promised that He would make of Abraham a great nation, and that through him all the families of the earth would be blessed (Gen. 12:1-5).

When Abraham reached Canaan, a *third* prophecy came, confirming that this was the land God would give his descendants (Gen. 12:7). Later, a *fourth* prophecy added details about how Abraham's nation would be as numerous as the dust of the earth, and how he had an immediate responsibility in the matter: He was to *look* and *walk* the length and breadth of the land (Gen. 13:14-17).

The *fifth* prophecy Abraham received, when he was about 83, gave a number of new insights into the who, what, when, where, and why of God's purposes and plans. The Lord said that Eliezer was unacceptable as Abraham's heir. He promised that his descendants would be as numerous as the stars. He told of Israel's coming bondage and exile, and how the fourth generation would eventually return to Canaan after four hundred years. Then God added details about the borders of the land and the nations that would be dispossessed (Gen. 15:1-21).

Further prophecy involving Abraham came to Hagar, Sarah's handmaiden, through an angel. God promised that her son would also give rise to a multitude. Then Ishmael was born (Gen. 16:1-16).

Next, when Abraham was 99, God spoke the *sixth* personal prophecy to him and added several new and important elements of His plan: Abraham was presented with new requirements (*"Be thou perfect"*), a new name (Abraham instead of Abram), a new covenant (circumcision), and a new prophetic increase (from the father of a great nation to the father of many nations). He also said for the first time explicitly that Sarah would be the mother of the promised seed—24 years after the original prophecy had been given (Gen. 17:1-21). When Abraham was one hundred years old, Isaac was finally born (Gen. 18:1-15). That same year God revealed to Abraham His intentions for Sodom and Gomorrah (Gen. 18:16-33).

Three years later, God spoke again to Abraham with clear instructions to cast out Hagar and Ishmael. God had done His part, and now Abraham had to do his (Gen. 21:9-21). Abraham received a total of 11 prophecies and the last one was the most challenging. After the *tenth* prophecy everything seemed to be settled for the next 22 years.

When Abraham was 125, however, God tested him by commanding him to sacrifice Isaac. When Abraham obeyed in faith, God transformed His conditional personal prophecy into an unconditional ratified oath. Abraham had passed all His tests of faith and obedience, and so the Lord swore by Himself that Abraham's prophecies would come to pass (Gen. 22:1-18). Yet another portion of God's word came to pass 50 years later, when Abraham died "in a good old age"—92 years after that particular prophecy had been spoken (Gen. 15:15; 25:7-11).

We can see from Abraham's life that many personal prophecies may be given over a lifetime for God to reveal His whole plan for a person's life. For that reason, time is often the greatest trial of faith for believing our prophecy. Abraham and Sarah had to wait patiently 25 years for the fulfillment of the prophecy about Isaac. David had to wait around 20 years for his kingship to be made manifest. And Joseph had to wait 22 years to see his dreams become reality.

Conditional vs. Unconditional Prophecy

From biblical examples we must conclude that prophecy is not always fulfilled. Some prophecies are *conditional*, with their fulfillment dependent on human behavior. Others are *unconditional* and will take place no matter what else happens.

Unconditional prophecy includes those divine decrees that are irrevocable. They will be fulfilled some day, some time, by some people; and not one devil in hell, not one human on earth, not one angel in Heaven can prevent God from making them come to pass. Unconditional prophecies are usually general rather than personal, though they may speak of specific people, places, and events. They refer to God's overall, ultimate plans and purposes for the human race that are dependent for their fulfillment, not on human behavior, but on God's unlimited power.

Typical of these prophecies is Daniel's prophetic interpretation of Nebuchadnezzar's dream. It predicted the rise and fall of several empires—Babylonian, Medo-Persian, Greek, and then Roman—and the coming of Christ and His Church Kingdom. This Kingdom, Daniel prophesied, would take dominion and reign forever over all the other kingdoms of the world. Because this is an unconditional prophecy about God's overall and ultimate plan for the world, we are guaranteed that it will come to pass. Though the antichrist will come, the saints will eventually fulfill God's predestined purpose for the Body of Christ, overcoming all the enemies of the Lord Jesus, and setting up God's Kingdom on earth (Dan. 2:44; 7:18,22,28; Rev. 2:26-27; 11:15; 12:10-11; 17:14; 19:11-21; 20:4-6).

Unconditional prophecies like these are certain to be fulfilled, but not necessarily by the person, people, or generation to whom they are originally given. For example, God's prophecy in the garden of Eden said that the seed of the woman would bruise the head of the serpent. Yet the fulfillment came not through Eve, but rather through Mary, thousands of years later.

God's final, unconditional prophetic oath to Abraham about the future ministry of his promised seed has also been fulfilled, but many of his descendants were not a part of the fulfillment because of their unbelief and wickedness. Others had to be used for the unconditional promise to come to pass. Several times Abraham's seed line through David was almost annihilated. But nothing could stop an unconditional, God-inspired prophecy from being fulfilled some time, some place, through some people.

God's unconditional judgment prophecies operate on a similar principle. The repentance of an individual or a generation may postpone such a prophecy, but it cannot cancel it. For example, God prophetically decreed destruction for the Assyrian empire, sending Jonah to prophesy the destruction of its capital, Nineveh, within 40 days. But all Nineveh repented, and so God changed His timetable, postponing the prophecy's fulfillment.

Even so, the repentance and belief in the prophecy were only temporary, and Nineveh eventually returned to its wickedness. So God reactivated the prophecy through the prophet Nahum, who told why and how the judgment was coming. Jonah's generation was spared, but just over a hundred years later, both Jonah's and Nahum's prophecies were fulfilled to the letter.

Another example is God's word to King Hezekiah of Judah (Isa. 38), through Isaiah, to *"set your house in order, for you are going to die."* The king begged earnestly for his life, and plea-bargained with God for more time. So God told the prophet to give a new prophecy that Hezekiah's death had been postponed 15 years. Yet in those years Hezekiah perpetrated ten horrible atrocities and judgments on Judah, and the judgment prophecy was finally fulfilled anyway, for Hezekiah died. Similar events took place with other kings, whose repentance only postponed judgment till another generation.

Unconditional prophecies, then, that relate God's overall purposes for His ultimate, universal plan for humanity can be fulfilled on time or postponed—according to man's response. But nothing can stop God from eventually fulfilling His predestined, prophesied purpose. Unconditional prophecies may be adjusted or rescheduled, but they cannot be cancelled, revoked, or stopped short of fulfillment.

Conditional prophecies, on the other hand, are those prophetic promises and declarations made by God to individuals that *can* be cancelled, altered, reversed, or diminished. They may fail and never be fulfilled. For prophecy of this kind to come to pass requires the proper participation and cooperation of the one who receives the prophetic word.

All personal prophecies are conditional, whether or not any conditions are made explicit. The Bible records many examples of this fact, such as God's prophecy to Moses in Exodus 6:6-8. At that time the Lord declared seven times *"I will"* with regard to Israel's liberation and possession of Canaan. No conditional wording ("I will...if you will...") was included in this prophecy. Yet it was fulfilled for only two men out of the six hundred thousand who received it. The prophecy was cancelled by the disobedience of all the others, so that the promise failed for more than a million and a half of the Israelites (Num. 13:26-33).

Two more examples from the Bible, a positive and a negative one, demonstrate that conditional prophecy depends upon our obedience. In both cases, the key word in God's evaluation of the man's response to prophecy was the word *because*. That word makes it clear that our right attitude and actions are the necessary conditions for the fulfillment of our personal prophecy.

We have seen how Abraham's prophecy was partial and progressive, expanding and unfolding over a lifetime. If we focus on the last prophetic pronouncements God gave him, we find that Abraham had actually passed a series of tests over the years that allowed God's purpose for him to be fully manifested. At each critical point where God called for obedience, Abraham had responded faithfully, even in his "final exam" when God asked him to sacrifice Isaac.

Notice carefully the wording of Abraham's last prophecy: *"**Now I know** that thou fearest God...By Myself have I sworn... for **because** thou hast done this thing, and hast not withheld thy son, thine only son...in thy seed shall all the nations of the earth be blessed, **because** thou hast obeyed My voice"* (Gen. 22:12,16-18, emphasis added). *Because* of Abraham's obedience, God made His conditional promise into an irrevocable, ratified oath as He swore by Himself to fulfill it.

The life of Saul provides a negative illustration of this same principle. Though he had been anointed king by the prophet Samuel, according to God's prophetic instructions (1 Sam. 9:15-10:8), Saul failed to hear God clearly, to follow through, and to obey completely God's directions. Saul's disobedience consequently negated the prophetic possibilities for his posterity.

God's rebuke through Samuel was explicit:

> *...Thou hast done foolishly: thou hast not kept the commandment* [personal prophecy] *of the Lord thy God, which He commanded thee: for now would the Lord have established thy kingdom upon Israel for ever. But* **now** *thy kingdom* [posterity] *shall not continue: the Lord hath sought Him a man after His own heart, and the Lord hath commanded him to be captain over His people,* **because** *thou hast not kept that which the Lord commanded thee* (1 Samuel 13:13-14).

Because Saul disobeyed, personal prophecy was annulled.

Rebellion against a prophetic word, Samuel said, is like the sin of witchcraft. Stubbornness in not following a prophetic word exactly is iniquity and idolatry (1 Sam. 15:23). This sin was so serious that even though Saul confessed it and repented, asking for forgiveness, the promise to his posterity was annulled. He was allowed to remain in his position as king, performing his ministry, for another 15 to 20 years. But the Holy Spirit had departed from him, and his royal anointing had been transferred to David rather than to his own children (1 Sam. 15:24-16:13).

Clearly, then, personal prophecies require *faith to fulfill* and *obedience to obtain*. The eleventh chapter of Hebrews repeatedly reminds us that the great men and women of faith did their mighty deeds and obtained their prophetic promises *"by faith."* But the Israelites who were faithless fell in the wilderness (Heb. 3:7-19; 4:1-2).

We can learn today from their example. When we receive our own personal prophecies, we must keep in mind that what God tells us will be partial, progressive, and conditional. Only if we cooperate with the Lord can we expect a fulfillment of what has been spoken to us. So next we must examine carefully how we can have the proper response to personal prophecy.

CHAPTER 14

RESPONDING PROPERLY TO PERSONAL PROPHECY

The biblical attitude toward prophecy is thoroughly positive. Not only are we told to avoid despising prophecy—that is, assigning to it a lesser role than is proper, we are also exhorted to prove all prophecies, and hold fast to what is good and accurate in them (1 Thess. 5:20-21). Even more importantly, God commands us to desire earnestly and *covet* the prophetic ministry (1 Cor. 12:31; 14:1,39). It is, in fact, the only ministry that the Scriptures tell Christians to covet.

When we begin to consider the benefits of personal prophecy, we can see why God places such importance on it. Both the gift of prophecy and the ministry of prophesying in the congregation are designed for edification, exhortation, and comfort (1 Cor. 14:3). The anointing and office of the prophet are intended to do even more: Prophets are able to give direction, instruction, correction, motivation, and impartation of gifts, and they deal with more specific areas of an individual's life, addressing him or her more personally. No wonder, then, that the Bible tells us to believe God's prophets, and we will prosper (2 Chron. 20:20).

One of the great blessings of personal prophecy is that it makes God more personal and real to the saints. When a prophet who knows nothing about us by natural means begins to prophesy, and the words that come out describe us and our situation exactly, we gain a new sense of God's reality and intimate concern. I have seen many people so hopelessly depressed that they were ready to give up ministry, or even give up serving God altogether. But as I began prophesying under the strong anointing of the Lord, describing exactly what they were going through and giving them the Lord's words of comfort and consolation, they were brought to a new place of hope and rejoicing. The tears would begin to flow as they realized that God really loved them and had not forsaken nor failed them. Despite circumstances and appearances, they were assured that all things were working together for their good.

Prophecy Produces Fruit of the Spirit— (Gal. 5:22)

The fruit of the Spirit is produced through the ministry of prophecy, and especially through the prophet's ministry of personal prophecy. It builds *faith*, makes God's *love* more real, and brings *peace* where there was once great anxiety and fear. It gives a vision of what God has planned for our lives, activating *hope*, which causes us not to be ashamed anymore.

The prophetic anointing imparts *grace* and *patience* for *endurance* and *longsuffering* until God's word is fulfilled in our lives. The Lord's personal prophetic promises of supernatural help and blessing overwhelm and fill us with God's *goodness* and *joy*. The presence of God and the word of God delivered bring conviction to us concerning any rebellion, sin, or complaining. In this way, the goodness of God leads us to *repentance*. And the words of divine wisdom, counsel, and instruction bring balance to our lives, enabling us to walk in *temperance*.

Even a personal prophecy about great ministry, accomplishments, and miracles, if it is truly God-anointed and given to someone properly prepared, does not lead to carnal pride. Instead, it brings a humble appreciation of God's working in us, and develops genuine *meekness*. In all these ways, then, personal prophecy can help cultivate the fruit of the Spirit in our lives.

Judging the Prophecy vs. Judging the Prophet

The Holy Spirit, not the preacher or prophet, has been commissioned with the responsibility of convicting of sin and convincing of righteousness. Yet both the prophet and the preacher have the responsibility to speak the truth in love. This quality is especially critical for the prophet; for while the preacher's ministry is usually viewed as a person speaking about God or for God, the words of the prophet are seen as God speaking through him.

Consequently, it brings more reproach on the nature and character of God for someone to prophesy "thus saith the Lord" with a bad attitude or delivery than it does for someone to preach with a wrong spirit or delivery. UnChristlike attitudes or behavior on the part of someone prophesying makes it more difficult to accept his or her prophetic word as from the Lord.

Recognizing the importance of prophesying in love, we must nevertheless learn to distinguish between judging a prophecy and judging the prophet if we are to respond correctly to God's word. We judge a *prophecy* by considering the content of the words spoken to determine whether they are true or false. We judge a *prophet* as a person by the quality of his life to discover whether he himself is a true or false prophet.

The difference becomes clear when we look at the case of a false prophet who prophesied a true word of the Lord. Balaam was such a man. He delivered true prophecies from God, and in fact gave the only Messianic prophecy in the Book of Numbers. Yet he was an unrighteous man in many ways.

We can judge the prophet himself by what I call the "Ten M's": manhood, ministry, message, maturity, marriage, methods, manners, money, morality, and motives. Though we cannot consider these individually here, we can note that few prophets, or ministers of any kind, have all of these life areas in perfect order and maturity. But when one of them is seriously out of order, a sensitive Christian will not have a full witness with the minister prophet.

When this happens, it is important not to let the prophet's personal problems rob us of a true word with which God wants to bless us. If we bear witness to what is said, God may be speaking a true word through him even though the man himself has needs in a particular personal area.

Infallibility and False Prophets

At the same time, we must not be quick to call someone a false prophet simply because something he said was inaccurate or did not seem to apply to us. The man may be honest, righteous, and upright, yet immature in his prophesying. He may have misinterpreted what the Lord was saying.

In this case we should say that he gave an inaccurate word or a false prophecy, but we cannot properly call him a false prophet unless we can prove that *the man himself* is false. Missing it a few times in prophecy does not make a false prophet. No mortal prophet is infallible; all are liable to make mistakes.

Prophets are usually placed in a difficult dilemma. If they were to claim infallibility, they would be denounced as heretics. Yet as soon as they demonstrate their fallibility by making a mistake, they are labeled false prophets.

We must remember, after all, that *all* mortals and their ministries are fallible. Jesus was and always will be the only man who was infallible; He perfectly represented the Father in word and deed 24 hours a day. He was given the fullness of Spirit without measure. All His teaching, counsel, and prophecies were in perfect accord with Heaven, and He embodied the fullness of all the ministries in the Church to come.

When Jesus ascended to Heaven, He divided His abilities into five categories of gifts to the Church: *"When He ascended upon high, He...gave gifts unto men...He gave some, apostles; and some, prophets; and some, evangelists; and some, pastors and teachers."* Each was given grace (unmerited divine enablement) *"according to the measure of the gift of Christ"* (Eph. 4:7-8,11).

All five of these are an extension of Christ's ministry to the Church. And all five are fallible, even though Christ Himself is not. Regardless of title, position, or years of experience, no minister ever reaches the position of infallibility. We all fail at times to minister the pure mind of Christ in our preaching, teaching, counseling, or prophesying.

For that reason, all ministers, prophets or otherwise, should be willing to admit their fallibility. If the pastor's counsel, the prophet's prophecy, or even a saint's word of knowledge proves to be inapplicable, unworkable, inaccurate, or nonsensical to the one who received it, then the minister of that word should be ready to acknowledge that he or she evidently missed it, or at least failed to interpret and apply properly the impressions received from the Holy Spirit.

False Prophet vs. False Prophecy

The prophet who misses it occasionally in his prophecies may be ignorant, immature, or presumptuous, or he may be ministering with too much zeal and too little wisdom and anointing. But this does not prove him a false prophet. If we were to judge true and false prophets solely by the accuracy of individual words they deliver, we would have to say that each time one gives a correct word he is a true prophet, and each time he is inaccurate he is a false prophet. That would mean that a prophet who ministers to 20 people during a service, speaking on target to one but not to another, would change from being a true prophet to a false prophet several times in one night! But a prophet does not change his status from mistakes in prophecy any more than a Christian changes his status from saved to unsaved every time he makes a mistake in his walk with the Lord.

It is certainly possible for a true prophet to be inaccurate. He would not do it knowingly, for a true prophet is so conscientious he would rather never speak at all than speak even one false word or give wrong directions to even one person. So we must understand the distinction between a false prophecy and a false prophet if we are to be open to what God says to us. One of the quickest ways to get in trouble with God is to falsely accuse one of Christ's true prophets. When we do that, we are touching the very nerve of Heaven, and we are sure to receive a negative reaction. God says in His Word, *"Do My prophets no harm"* (1 Chron. 16:22).

More True Prophets Than False

In my 35 years of experience with prophets and personal prophecy, I have met only two ministers that I would publicly call false prophets—and they did not claim to be prophets. (I am speaking here of people within the Church, not the representatives of false cults or antichrist groups that are not Christian.) I have also been around scores of women ministers who prophesy, but I only knew one whom I would consider a false prophetess.

This particular woman is a good example of what a false prophet can be like. She was what I would call a "charismatic witch": a woman who professes to be born again and to speak in tongues, proclaiming basic charismatic doctrine—yet who uses her "prophesying" to manipulate people for selfish purposes. This woman would say "thus saith the Lord," and then speak words to control others around her. She and her husband had about 20 young people who really loved the Lord and thought they were doing God's will and work. But they were actually pawns in this woman's power.

Charismatic Witchcraft—Prophetic Manipulation

Samuel declared that when anyone manipulates prophecy for his or her own gain, that person is guilty of the sin of witchcraft (1 Sam. 15:22-23). When anyone uses prayer or prophecy to control others according to their own will rather than God's will, by biblical standards they are actually guilty of the sin or spirit of witchcraft. God does not answer such prayers or confirm such prophecies, but the devil can use the words prayed or spoken as fiery darts to harass and oppress true children of God.

If you should find yourself being prayed or prophesied against in this way for the purpose of selfish manipulation, do not respond in kind. Instead, pray this prayer: "Father, in Jesus' name I renounce whatever they are praying or speaking against me." You can neutralize any negative words spoken against you by practicing the New Testament principles propagated in Matthew 5:44; Luke 6:28; Romans 12:14; First Corinthians 4:12.

Despite the occasional false prophet we encounter, we should not let the counterfeit keep us from receiving the genuine. There cannot be counterfeit money unless there is government-produced real money. There cannot be false prophets and counterfeit prophecies unless there are God-ordained prophets and true prophecies. Find the real prophets and receive the benefits of true personal prophecies. The percentage of false prophets is certainly much lower than the devil would have us believe. Out of the six hundred pages of personal prophecy I have received over the years, only two were absolutely false, and perhaps were a person's own opinion rather than God's word to me. But I am more than willing to put up with the fraction of a percent that are bad in order to receive the overwhelming majority that are God-inspired. We must not let a few negative experiences with the prophetic realm allow us to grieve the Holy Spirit and sin against the command of Scripture that says *"despise not prophesying."*

CHAPTER 15

MAJOR DECISIONS AND GEOGRAPHICAL MOVES

Prophets and personal prophecy have played major roles in the decisions and activities of God's people throughout the Bible. The decision of the children of Israel to make a major move from Egypt to Canaan was made based on a personal prophecy from Prophet Moses to them. The Bible also records that some people made decisions based on supposed personal prophecy that ended in tragedy because it was not a true word from the Lord (1 Kings 22:6).

For that reason, all of the guidelines for personal prophecy must be observed before taking action to buy, sell, move, or make a major decision in any field. We must incorporate all the principles of the "three W's" of the Word, will, and way. Especially important are the five or six methods of knowing and confirming the will of God on the matter, and the numerous things that must happen before the way can be worked out. We should never take final action until the will and way have been confirmed fully.

"Spooky Spiritual" Christians

Christians need to be led by the Holy Spirit and be inspired, motivated, and directed by *rhemas* and personal prophecy.

But that does not eliminate our need to live and function as natural human beings. Being led of the Spirit and participating in personal prophecy does not mean that we must become "spooky spiritual." That is, we must not become "more heavenly minded than earthly good," with more zeal than wisdom. We must avoid being hyper-faith or "charis-maniacs" who are unbalanced in scriptural understanding, spiritually immature, and emotionally unstable.

We should remember that prophets, personal prophecy, and gifts of the Holy Spirit do not make "spooky spiritual" saints—they just reveal them. Rain does not make weeds; it just causes whatever is in the ground to sprout. Pressure on an object does not make weak spots; it just uncovers them.

Spooky Spirituals—Who, What, and How?

The Bible college I attended years ago developed some "spooky spirituals." One prophet came to chapel and said that God told him to prophesy to a person who had a certain color and style of clothing. Another one said God showed him he was to minister to those who had fasted breakfast. After a few of these prophetic happenings, several of the students felt they had to get a word from the Lord concerning what style and color of clothes they wore that day. They had to get a word about what meals to eat, whether to go to work, and on and on.

"Spooky spirituals" become convinced that they need a special *rhema* word from the Lord to do even natural, everyday activities which should be done by the common sense God programmed within the human soul. Supernatural knowledge is only needed and given by God when natural knowledge and ability are insufficient. God did not make robots or humanoids, but rather human beings in His own image and likeness with a mind and will to think and act. Most of the Christian life can be lived in harmony with God's will by following the Bible and exercising God-given, natural common sense and ability.

"Spooky spirituals" are also those who think they have to have certain sensations, vibrations, and manifestations in their flesh and emotions to be "in the Spirit." They become a little weird or way out into some strange realm. It is true that psychics and spiritualists must concentrate, meditate, and project themselves into a mental and emotional trance to receive and give supernatural insight about people and things. But this is not necessary for Christians who have the mind of Christ abiding within. Our faith operates from the Spirit, not from an emotional psychic function.

I was among old-time Pentecosts in my early years, and it was the general attitude among them that to be "in the Spirit" you had to be very emotional about it. If you could control what you were doing, it was not God. Because of this, many sincere, born-again, Spirit-baptized Christians became a little "spooky spiritual" when they sensed God's presence, praised the Lord, or moved in gifts of the Holy Spirit. I am not speaking here of the unusual manifestations that may accompany a sovereign move of God in a service, but rather those habitual attitudes and actions people grow to expect as confirmations of God's anointing and their own spirituality. Yet we do not have to become a "spooky spiritual" to manifest supernatural gifts and God's mighty power and presence, or to live and walk in the Spirit.

True Spiritual *Rhemas* for Making Major Decisions

Numerous testimonies could be given about prophetic words that were given directly from God, from prophets, or from prophetic presbyteries that dealt with someone's major decisions, geographical moves, or buying and selling. One such incident happened to some close friends of ours. They had just arrived at Yellowstone National Park and spent a few hours getting their camp all set up. Just as they settled in for the night, the wife kept getting an uneasy feeling in the pit of her stomach, and the words kept coming, "Pack up and move out of this camp tonight." They prayed about it, and the feeling and the words came stronger to her.

The husband realized that they were not going to get any rest anyway as long as his wife felt this way, and besides, he was beginning to feel the same way. So they packed everything back up and about midnight moved to find another campsite. That night a great rock slide took place and buried that campsite under several feet of rock and mud. Their lives depended upon their overcoming human reasoning and obeying their rhema to make a geographical move.

Personal Prophecy Reveals God's Place and Purpose

I once prophesied over several people while ministering at a church in Indiana. The prophetic word told one man that he was not to make a move he was contemplating. I did not know him at all or that he was getting ready to move the next week to Chicago. His pastor had already counseled him that he did not believe it was the will of God for him to move, so based on these two words he did not move.

A little later the same man had a job transfer to California. He called me from there a few months later, asking for a word from the Lord as to what he should do, because nothing was going right with his family or job. I asked him if he had written out his prophecy that I had given to him at his home church in Indiana, and if he had it with him. He did, so he read it to me over the phone.

The third page of the prophecy had these thoughts: "Here is where you will bud, blossom, and become fruitful...Do not leave because of pressure...If you do leave, you will have to come right back to where you left from...for this is the place where I want you to grow, mature, and minister for me." I said, "Brother, it sounds like you have no alternative but to move back to Indiana if you want the blessing of being in God's will."

If we receive a prophetic word from a proven prophet, and our pastor witnesses to it, we too had better seriously consider doing what the prophet prophesies and the pastor counsels. *"Obedience is better than sacrifice"* (1 Sam. 15:22).

CHAPTER 16

GUIDELINES FOR HANDLING PERSONAL PROPHECY

Certain responses in attitude and action are necessary for us to appropriate the maximum benefits of a personal prophecy. When a personal prophecy is a true *rhema* from the Lord, the proper biblical principles must be practiced for the word to be effective and productive. Whether we receive a promise from the *Logos* or from a *rhema*, the same response is required on our part to obtain what is promised.

The following principles for proper response are intended especially for personal prophecies received verbally through a prophet or prophetic presbytery. But they can also be applied to any of the other various ways God communicates His thoughts to an individual.

Record, Read, and Meditate on Your Personal Prophecies

The apostle Paul told Timothy: *"Neglect not the gift that is in thee, which was **given thee by prophecy**, with the laying on of the hands of the presbytery. Meditate upon these things; give thyself wholly to them; that thy profiting may appear to all"* (1 Tim. 4:14-15, emphasis added). Here he reminded Timothy that the young man had been given a gift by prophecy when he was prophesied over by the prophetic presbytery. Timothy was told not to neglect this gift, but rather to meditate over his personal prophecies so that everything spoken would be made manifest and become profitable to the whole Body of Christ.

How could Timothy properly meditate upon the prophecies unless they were written down for him to read over again? And how can *we* meditate on our personal prophecies unless we record them as well?

Many of the prophecies I received in the 1950s and early '60s were not recorded because of the lack of sound-recording equipment at the time. Bulky, large-reel recorders were all we had available, so the words I did get on tape were recorded twice, first on a seven-inch-reel wire recorder, and then on a seven-inch-tape reel. Finally they were written out by hand, and then typed.

Modern Inventions for New Ministries. Not until the mid '60s did cassette recorders become plentifully available. Just as God brought about the invention of the printing press to spread the truths of the Reformation, I believe God brought about the creation of the cassette player in time to provide an abundance of fast and easy sound recording for the restoration of prophetic ministry. We can be grateful today that such convenient recording equipment is available, and we should always make use of it for taping personal prophecy.

A word from God that is spoken but not retained on tape or in writing becomes of little value, because the important details are soon forgotten. The mind can remember only a little of the exact wording of a prophecy, especially if it is long. I know this from personal experience; of the thousands of words that were spoken to me prophetically but never recorded, I can only recall two or three phrases. We simply cannot expect to respond properly to a personal prophecy unless all the words are recorded, read, and understood clearly.

Proper Preparation for Personal Prophecy. For that reason, we should observe the following procedure for recording personal prophecies. First, if at all possible, proper preparation should be made for a sound recording of prophecies. When an experienced prophetic presbytery is ministering, they will normally make arrangements to record everything.

If someone approaches us saying he or she has a word from the Lord for us, we should ask them to wait a moment until we can get a recorder, or have them come with us to a place where there is recording equipment. If no equipment is available, we can ask the one who believes he or she has a word to write it out so we can retain it and derive the full benefits of it. Though this may involve a little work, a true man or woman of God will honor this request without resentment or offense.

If the word is given from a platform by a prophet or someone flowing in the gift of prophecy, we must write down everything we can remember, trying to get at least the main points. I have had to record several prophecies this way, and even though the exact wording was lost, the main thoughts could be preserved and compared with other prophecies I had received.

Recording Gives Comparison and Confirmation. After we record several prophecies and compare them, we usually notice that some of the same thoughts and words appear from the messages of different individuals who were not familiar with what was said to us before. This agreement in prophecies helps us realize that they must really be the word of the Lord, because they are being confirmed in the mouth of several witnesses.

In the Bible, when God wanted to emphasize a point, He inspired the writers to use the same words or phrases several times. The same is true when God inspires a prophet to give us a personal word. His emphasized thoughts will be repeated several times in a prophecy, and the Holy Spirit will cause others to prophesy the same thoughts at other times and places. This is important when we must make a major decision based on prophecy, because it is better to decide such matters only on the authority of several confirmations.

Two Reasons for Recording. In my ministry I insist that every personal prophecy be recorded, for two reasons.

The first is the one we have mentioned: for the benefit of the person receiving the prophecy. Much of what is said, even if it is remembered in the days following, will not become meaningful until months or even years later. At the same time, the only things that tend to register with us when prophecies are being spoken are those things that are relevant to our current circumstances. When we read the prophecy over again during a later chapter of our life, we usually notice many details we did not remember being spoken. So to give someone a long, flowing prophecy without recording can be a waste of time for everyone involved. All that will be of benefit is the spiritual impartation and charge received from the prophet.

The second reason I insist that all prophecies be recorded is for the personal protection of the prophet. People have a way of misapplying, twisting, and reinterpreting what they hear, and think they hear in a prophecy, so that what they remember conforms to their selfish desires instead of God's will.

A Life Experience. A good example of this problem comes from an experience I once had when ministering in a church with an unmarried pastor. I prophesied to a young single woman in the congregation, who several weeks later told Jane, my daughter-in-law, "Did you know that Dr. Hamon prophesied I would marry my pastor?" Jane questioned her statement, and asked whether she had written the prophecy out. She had, and when the woman showed it to Jane, it read: "God will give you the desires of your heart." Her desire, said the young lady, was to marry her pastor! Jane, of course, had to advise her that she could not assume any marriage plans; but if the prophecy had not been written down, convincing her of that might have been more difficult.

First Interpretation Is Not Always a True Application. Recording, writing out, and meditating on prophecies also helps us realize that several interpretations may be possible for the same words. We cannot assume that an unspecific prophecy applies to a particular situation. Once, for example, I went to a minister for prophecy, extending my faith for an assurance that God would supply a desperate financial need.

It was two days after a $40,000 payment was due. The prophecy I received said, "I will supply your need, for to deny you would be to deny Myself."

I went away confessing that my financial need was met, but it never was. So I went to the Lord and told Him that He did not fulfill His prophetic promise to me. But God replied, "Yes, I did. I met the need I promised prophetically through my servant. *You* thought your greatest need was that payment, but I saw a greater need than that money, and I have met it faithfully." He then enlightened my mind so I could see how much greater was the need He *did* meet that night. In light of this example and many others, we should always go over a recorded word from God with a pastor or elder who believes in and understands personal prophecy. That person can help us make sure that we are not misinterpreting or misapplying the message.

Another reason for recording prophecy is that we should not make any major decision based on it, or draw any final conclusions about what it means, while it is being given. It is best just to listen attentively and prayerfully, reserving all final judgments for later when we have the prophecy before us in written form. Then we can follow the proper procedures for judging and evaluating the prophecy. Our emotional, mental, and physical posture while receiving a prophecy is simply not conducive to proper evaluation. At that time, our spirit is better engaged in witnessing actively to the spirit of the person prophesying and the divine inspiration which is motivating him or her.

Witness to Your Prophecy

How do we bear witness with a prophetic word's accuracy in spirit and content? The same way we bear witness that we are a child of God: *"The Spirit itself beareth witness with our spirit..."* (Rom. 8:16). We *prove* prophecy by biblical principles and the proper criteria for judging prophetic words, but we *witness* to prophecy with our *spirit*.

I have sometimes heard people say, "I did not witness with that prophecy." But after questioning them, I discovered that what they actually meant was that the prophecy did not fit their theology, or they did not like what was said, or their emotions reacted negatively to it. They failed to understand that we do not bear witness with the soulish mind, emotions, or will, according to personal opinions, desires, or goals.

Discerning Between Soul and Spirit. The *spirit realm* of man is where divine love and faith operate. The emotions are in the soul. Our five senses, including feeling, are in the natural flesh realm.

Our reasoning is in the mind, not the spirit. So our traditions, beliefs, and strong opinions are not true witnesses to prophetic truth. In fact, these parts of us often bring doubt, confusion, resentment, rejection, and rebellion against true personal prophecy. Our head may say, "No" while our heart says, "Go." Our soul may say, "I don't understand," while our spirit says, "It's fine; don't lean to your own understanding."

Spirit Witness vs. Personal Belief. Consider, for example, what would happen if a devoted Catholic received a prophecy saying he was not to worship Mary. He would probably not feel right about that word because of his tradition and his emotional tie to Mary. In the same way, if you prophesied water baptism by immersion to a Presbyterian or speaking in tongues to a traditional Baptist, you would receive much the same reaction.

Most people cannot discern between a negative soulish reaction and the spirit's lack of witness to something. The spirit reaction originates deep within our being. Many Christians describe the physical location of its corresponding sensation as a feeling in the upper stomach or lower chest area. A negative spirit-witness, with a message of either "No," "Be careful," or "Something's not right," usually manifests itself with a nervous, jumpy, or uneasy feeling, a deep, almost unintelligible sensation that something is not right.

This sensation can only be trusted when we are more in tune with our spirit than with our thoughts. If our thinking is causing these sensations, then it could be a soulish reaction rather than the spirit bearing a negative witness.

When the spirit is giving a positive witness, or more specifically, when God's Spirit is bearing witness with our spirit that a prophetic word is right, is of God, and is according to His divine will and purpose, then our spirit reacts with the fruit of the Holy Spirit. There is a deep, unexplainable peace and joy, a warm, loving feeling, or even a sense of our spirit jumping up and down with excitement. This good, positive, assuring sensation lets us know that the Holy Spirit is bearing witness with our spirit that everything is in order, even though we may not understand all that is being said, or the soul may not be able to adjust immediately to all the thoughts being presented.

Don't Do What You Don't Witness To. If there is neither reaction nor sensation in the spirit, but rather more of a neutral feeling, then it is a "wait and see" situation. The spirit is saying, "Nothing to get excited about, nothing to get worried about." Time will tell, so we must trust and obey, believe and become, desire and do what we know to do. If the prophecy is of God, it will all come to pass, and we will fulfill God's will.

New Revelation vs. Confirmation. We should note here as well one other important principle of bearing witness to a personal prophecy. It has to do with the issue of *new revelation* as opposed to *confirmation* in a prophetic word.

Sadly enough, someone at sometime for some reason known only to himself began teaching that prophecy is only for confirmation. In its current form, this teaching insists that we should reject any personal prophecy that presents a thought that is totally new to us. It claims that God will only speak in prophecy things we have already heard from Him in our own spirit, serving merely as confirmation. This is the ideal, but not the real.

I would agree that prophecy is received and born witness to more easily and immediately when it is a confirmation of things that have already been considered by the person who is given the prophecy. But I also believe we are seeking a false sense of security when we insist that God will never have a prophet tell us anything unless He has told us first. In fact, I think we are indulging ourselves in a proud ego trip to claim that God must always speak to us first, personally, before He can speak to us through someone else. No Scripture supports such a belief.

Prophets Speak Things Never Perceived by the Person. On the contrary, there are several scriptural illustrations revealing that a prophet *can* speak new things to a person from God which that person had never before thought of or considered. In the case of *David*, for example, we have a young shepherd boy anointed by Samuel with a prophecy that he would become king. We have no indication that this young man had ever before even dreamed of ruling Israel.

Elisha was a farmer with no thought of going into the ministry until Elijah revealed that he would be a prophet. *Jehu* had no idea that he might someday be king of Israel until Elijah revealed it to him. We have no indication that *Hazael* had thought about being king of Syria until Elisha prophesied it. *Paul* received his first insight that he would be an apostle to the Gentiles, not from Jesus on the road to Damascus nor from the inward voice of the Holy Spirit, but rather from Ananias when he prophesied the word of the Lord and ministered healing to him.

We cannot reject the word of a prophet or consider it inaccurate simply because we have not already been thinking about what is prophesied. God uses the prophets to speak new truth, not only to the Church, but to individuals as well. We must prove all words before we reject them.

Present-day Portrayal. I once gave a prophetic word to a man who was in the oil business that he would go into a new business and have a chain of restaurants. At the time, such a move had never even entered his mind. So for four years he stayed in the oil business and forgot about the prophecy. But when the oil business went bad, an opportunity opened up for him to go into the restaurant business—and he is now opening his third restaurant in that chain.

If we receive totally new thoughts in personal prophecy, our best response is to write them out, consider them, and pray about them. Then we should wait and see, and remain open, teachable, and divinely flexible. When God opens the door of opportunity in the area described, we will already have a confirmation that He is in it. Prophetic confirmations sometimes come before we even know we need one.

War a Good Warfare With Prophecy

Paul told Timothy to do more than meditate on his prophecies; he said they should be used to fight the battle: *"This charge I commit unto thee, son Timothy, **according to the prophecies which went before on thee**, that thou by them mightest war a good warfare"* (1 Tim. 1:18, emphasis added).

Can we, too, take the personal prophecies we have witnessed to and proven, and wage spiritual warfare with them? Yes! The kings of Judah and Israel such as David and Jehoshaphat defeated their enemies based on personal prophecies they received from a prophet.

Jehoshaphat actually followed specific directions for a battle plan given by a prophetic utterance. He went forth to war with full confidence that he would win because of the prophecy given by Jahaziel. The king believed the prophet had given him the right word of direction, which in turn inspired his faith in his God, who had inspired the prophet to speak. In this way he defeated a mighty enemy host, and laid down one of the greatest principles of proper response to prophets and personal prophecy: *"Believe in the Lord your God, so shall ye be established; believe His prophets, so shall ye prosper"* (2 Chron. 20:20b).

A prophetic word such as Jehoshaphat's, which gave battle strategy that would only work because God said to do it that way at that particular time, is rightly called a personal prophecy. Like the word to Joshua at Jericho, it was individual and unique. The methods that Jehoshaphat and Joshua used on these occasions would not go into a war manual as standard procedure for winning a battle. And we have no record that anyone else was ever told by God to destroy a city by marching around its walls, or to conquer several armies by sending singers and musicians out ahead of the soldiers and artillery. These battles were won because the leaders followed specific directions from the Lord for a specific occasion.

Personal Prophecy Gives Power to Persevere. The apostle Paul was able to endure great suffering with joy because the man of God had prophesied to him that it was God's will for him to suffer for the name of Christ Jesus. Prophecy by Ananias first put the thought in his spirit and mind that he would become an apostle to the Gentiles. Then a rhema from the Lord assured him that God's grace was sufficient for any problem or suffering he faced. Finally, a personal word from the Lord that he must go to Rome gave him the courage to fight the good fight of faith until he finished his course at Rome.

Power of Personal Prophecy Proved Personally. A good example of waging war with prophecy comes from the experience of my wife, Evelyn. In 1979 a prophet gave her a word that contained some things she had not previously thought of, yet she believed the prophet and prospered; she believed God and saw things established.

Part of the prophecy declared that God had made a covenant with her that our children could not and would not marry out of the Lord's will. At the time our two youngest children were not married. Our oldest son, Tim, was already married, and we had all felt an assurance and a witness that Karen was the right one for him. But our second son, 20-year-old Tom, was going steady with a Christian girl that both my wife and I felt was not the right one. At the same time, Sherilyn, our 18-year-old daughter, was planning to marry a solid Christian young man.

Sherilyn's fiancé was like a son to us, and we could find no scriptural fault with him. But my wife could not get peace about their marriage.

Same Wedding But Different Groom. After a summer of itinerate ministry, we all ended up back in Phoenix, Arizona, where we lived at the time, and we went ahead and had the wedding—but with a different groom!

Meanwhile, Tom had broken off his steady relationship with that young lady, had met another beautiful blonde in Bible college, and became engaged to her. I am convinced that their eventual marriage resulted in part because Evelyn had done warfare with her prophecy.

Yes, we can take our proven personal prophecy as a word from the Lord and war a warfare with it that will cause everything to work according to the perfect will of God. If we believe God, we will be established, but we must also believe His prophets in order to prosper.

Do Nothing Differently Unless Definitely Directed

Unless God gives us explicit instructions to act upon, the proper response to personal prophecy is simply to continue doing what we have been doing before we received the word of the Lord. This is true even if we have been told of great things we will do in the future.

David was called in from tending the sheep, and Samuel anointed him to be king over all Israel. But there were no prophetic indications about when or how this was to come about, nor any instructions for David to follow. It was simply a prophetic proclamation.

So David returned to his ministry of tending sheep, practicing with his slingshot, and learning to sing and play music to the Lord. Since he was in his early teens at the time, there was nothing he could do about his personal prophecy of kingship except to wait upon God's timing and to occupy his time profitably while he dreamed about his day of prophetic fulfillment. For all true prophecies of future accomplishments—ours as well—God's time for fulfillment must be awaited.

On the other hand, when a prophecy is received that includes specific instructions and an anointing for immediate action, then it is time to act upon the prophecy. Jehu, one of the chief captains of the army of Israel, received such a prophecy. Elisha commissioned one of his young prophets to take a box of anointing oil and go to Ramoth-Gilead, where he was to anoint Jehu king of Israel, and then run. The young man not only anointed Jehu king, but he also prophesied the destruction of the Ahab dynasty, which Elijah had also prophesied to Jehu some 12 years earlier.

Take Action Immediately When Specifically Directed. When Jehu told his fellow captains what the prophet had said and done, they immediately crowned him king. Jehu believed that the time was right, and his comrades agreed. So he drove his chariot furiously to Jezreel and slaughtered Ahab's household. Then he continued on to Samaria, destroyed the same way there, and killed all the prophets of Baal.

Jehu's years of experience had prepared him for this time. He was zealous for the Lord, willing and ready. All his fellow captains witnessed with his decision. So God's timing caused everything to fall in order, enabling and encouraging him to act immediately upon the prophecy and to follow through until he had fulfilled faithfully all that had been spoken (2 Kings 9-10).

Jehu, then, *took action immediately* to fulfill his prophecy and was launched into a 28-year reign as king of Israel. David *did nothing immediately* to fulfill his prophecy, but waited patiently about 17 years before it was even partially fulfilled, and another seven before fulfillment was complete. His patient waiting without trying to make the prophecy come to pass on his own strength ultimately launched him into a successful kingship ministry of 40 years.

From these two biblical examples we can conclude that it is not enough to receive a prophecy. We must also respond properly. We must meditate on it, witness to it, wage warfare with it, and act only if specifically directed to do so. Next, we must consider the attitudes necessary to have personal prophecy come to pass.

CHAPTER 17

ATTITUDES OF A PROPER RESPONSE TO PROPHECY

A truly inspired personal prophecy is God's specific word to an individual. So the same scriptural principles for the proper attitudes toward the written *Logos* Word should apply equally to the prophetically spoken *rhema* word. Several attitudes are critical for receiving a personal prophecy properly:

Faith

Faith is absolutely essential for receiving anything from God. If we intend to receive personal prophecy from a presbytery or a prophet, we should evaluate fully those who might minister prophetically to us. If we conclude that they are qualified, competent men and women of God, then the prophecies should be received in confidence, believing that word to be true and factual.

Hebrews 4:2 tells us about the Israelites in the wilderness that *"the word preached did not profit them, not being mixed with faith in them that heard it."* If the Gospel, which is the power of God, could not profit, how much more so is that true when a present-day prophet speaks a word from the Lord.

If a prophetic word is received with an attitude of acceptance and faith, then the rhema that is heard will create faith for the fulfillment of that word: *"So then faith cometh by hearing, and hearing by the word [rhema] of God"* (Rom. 10:17). Faith is the procurer of all God's prophetic promises. Without faith it is impossible to please God, but with faith in God all things are possible (Heb. 11:6; Mark 9:23; 1 John 5:4).

Obedience

True faith will be accompanied by the work of obedience. If our hearing does not progress to the point of our doing, we become a candidate for deception, as James tells us: *"Be ye doers of the word, and not hearers only, deceiving your own selves"* (James 1:22).

The Lord speaks a prophetic word to us, not just to tickle our intellect, but to bring the understanding necessary to *do* the will of God: *"Those things which are revealed belong unto us and to our children forever, that we may **do** all the **words** of this law"* (Deut. 29:29, emphasis added). The same principle that applied to the children of Israel receiving the word of the law apply to a person receiving words of instruction in personal prophecy: *"For not the hearers of the law are just before God, but the doers of the law shall be justified"* (Rom. 2:13).

Better to Not Know Than Know and Not Do. *"Therefore to him that knoweth to do good, and doeth it not, to him it is sin"* (James 4:17). It is better not to receive a word at all than to receive one and then not do what the word says to do. But if we obey and do exactly what the word says, then we deliver ourselves from deception and open our spirit and mind to know the will of God. Jesus said, *"If any man will do God's will, he shall know...whether it be of God..."* (John 7:17). So if we believe and do what we know to do, Christ will speak and reveal more concerning His Word, will, and way.

The proper response to personal prophecy thus requires obedience, a cooperation with the word that allows it to have room in our lives for the fulfillment of God's will: *"Let the word of Christ dwell in you richly in all wisdom"* (Col. 3:16). We need to pray the prayer that Paul requested: *"Pray for us, that the word of the Lord may have free course"* (2 Thess. 3:1).

Patience

Hebrews 6:12 reminds us that it is with faith *and patience* that the promises are inherited. These two qualities enable us to appropriate the prophetic words until the promise is secured.

After we have received a personal prophecy, and proven it to be a true word from the Lord, we must maintain a constant faith and confidence that it will come to pass regardless of the time required—and that requires patiently pursuing God's will. Once we are convinced that a word is a true *rhema*, we must allow no one to rob us of it.

Personal Prophecy Almost Destroyed. I did not understand this principle when I received my prophecies from a presbytery at the age of 19. After leaving college I settled among Christians who were not familiar with either the prophetic presbytery or personal prophecy. Discouragement came because nothing was happening as quickly as I had expected.

I showed the prophecy to a couple of ministers and a friend. They all said they did not witness to it and believed it was a bondage to me. They suggested that I burn it.

In a moment of confusion and discouragement I was ready to cast the prophecies into the flames and destroy all record of their contents. But thank God they were not destroyed, for every one of them has come to pass. They have been a constant source of inspiration, encouragement, and motivation over the last 35 years.

Personal Prophecies Are Precious Pearls. When Jesus said not to cast pearls before swine, (Matt. 7:6) He was referring to the Pharisees. He was telling us not to take something God has given us and expose it to religious leaders who do not believe God speaks in personal prophecy today. The devil can use well-meaning ministers and Christian friends to rob us of our word from the Lord, but we must not let them.

Our personal prophecies may presently be causing us confusion and frustration. They may be discouraging because what was promised is not happening in the time and way we think it should. They may contradict everything that is now in our life and circumstances. But we must nevertheless wait patiently upon the Lord, and He will fulfill His prophetic word, changing both us and our circumstances. If we press on, privately and patiently pursuing our rhema from the Lord, we will eventually possess all our prophetic promises. Every true word from God will come to pass in His predestined purpose and timing.

Patience Necessary for Persevering During Prophetic Process. God's process for prophetic fulfillment is rarely sooner than we expect. It is almost always later, and sometimes much later. When I first came out of college I expected to be launched into worldwide ministry because of the prophecies over me. I expected all those glowing words about being "a leader of leaders" to become an instant reality. Having been given a promise of "the gifts of the Spirit and the faith of God, the ministry of deliverance and anointing to bring the Body of Christ together, and prophetic anointing," I fully believed they would be manifested immediately. And I was full of zeal, vision, dedication, and determination.

In 1953, the president of the Bible college where I was attending asked me to testify on his nationwide radio program. My testimony at that time is an indication of how inflamed I was with the vision that our generation had to take the gospel to all the world: "This world," I said, "is just so big. The devil is on it and I am on it. Both of us cannot stay. One of us has to leave and I am giving notice to the devil that it's not going to be me."

Wrong Perception Brings Pressure and Impatience. I and many other ministers like me were convinced that Jesus was coming any moment. We had no time to waste. I definitely believed that Jesus would return before I turned 30. We could only think in terms of months, not years. Waiting and patience was not part of our vocabulary then; everything had to be done today because there was not going to be a tomorrow.

Did God listen to my prayers telling Him how His imminent return made it necessary for Him to make me the greatest, doing the most, immediately? Yes, He heard me, but He did not take me seriously or get all shaken up. He knew His own timetable, and the growing process that would be necessary before all of those prophecies could become manifest in their full demonstration. God is never in a hurry, but He is always on time. God is not motivated by intimidation or frustration.

I was fasting several days a month and praying by the hour every day that God's purpose would be perfected in me. And how did He answer my pleas, prayers, and persistence? By placing me as the pastor of a small church in the Yakima Valley of Washington State.

I was a southern boy from Oklahoma stuck in the cold, unfamiliar territory of the Northwest. And the church I took there had a history of problems. Several years before, it had experienced continuous revival every night for four years. Almost every person in that small town of five thousand had been in that church at one time or another. But the pastor had died a few years before I arrived, and the congregation had been dwindling away. The church had split several times over almost every controversial issue in Christendom. So the roaring fire of revival had swept by, leaving only ashes and a few smoldering embers by the time I arrived.

The 25 or 30 saints who had weathered all those storms were singing, "I shall not be, I shall not be moved"—and they meant it in every way. They had seen it all, been through it all, and knew it all. So they voted in a young pip-squeak prophet to be their pastor with the idea that after all they had been through they could put up with this young man until he matured some.

Mature Man Must Be Made Before the Mighty Ministry Is Manifested. The purpose of God kept me there six years. God was making the man before He could manifest the ministry fully. As with all of us, the ministry could be no greater than the man. If it were, the immature man would be crushed, because we must be properly prepared to carry the full weight of mature ministry.

Even with Jesus, God took thirty years of life on earth for preparation, and only three for ministry—a ten-to-one ratio. David had a similar life: 24 years of preparation led up to the fulfillment of his prophecy about ministry. Joseph's prophetic dream did not come true until 22 years later, and Noah had to work on the ark one hundred years before it was ready to float on the flood.

Biblical Principles for Procuring Personal Prophecies. In Psalm 37:7-11 we have a clear biblical admonition for the proper response to personal prophecy, especially those areas that speak of our ministry and the things to be accomplished:

> *Rest in the Lord, and wait patiently for Him. Commit your way* [the way for your personal prophecies to be fulfilled] *unto the Lord; trust also in Him and He shall bring it* [your personal prophecy] *to pass. Fret not thyself because of him who prospereth in his way* [the person whose ministry is already being fully manifested], *because of the man who bringeth wicked devices to pass* [the minister who is prosperous and successful, yet not righteous in all his ways, doing things his way rather than God's]. *Cease from anger* [at God for not coming through when you wanted Him to], *and forsake wrath* [release your frustrations and self-imposed pressure to perform before God's time]. *For those that wait upon the Lord and the meek shall inherit the earth and delight themselves in the abundance of peace.*

Other Scriptures are equally as clear. *"Cast not away therefore your confidence, which hath great recompense of reward. For ye have **need of patience**, that, **after ye have done the will** of God, ye might receive the promise* [personal prophetic promise] *of God"* (Heb. 10:35-36, emphasis added). *"Wait on the Lord: be of good courage, and He shall strengthen thine heart: wait, I say, on the Lord"* (Ps. 27:14). *"They that wait upon the Lord shall renew their strength; they shall mount up with wings as eagles; they shall run, and not be weary; and they shall walk, and not faint"* (Isa. 40:31). Teach us, Lord, to wait! Waiting upon the Lord for our prophecies to come to pass demonstrates not only *patience*, but also *faith* and *obedience*.

Humility, Meekness, and Submission

When we receive a true word of prophecy and respond with pride, anger, doubt, resentment, criticism, self-justification, or arrogance, we reveal immaturity or a wrong spirit. The result is that our attitude neutralizes much of what God wants to accomplish by the words spoken. For that reason, it is critical that we receive the prophetic utterance in a spirit of humility, meekness, and submission.

Sometimes we have preconceptions about a great ministry we believe God will confirm and describe through the prophet. When God does not confirm our ideas of great self-importance, then we may become disillusioned, depressed, and angry at God and the one prophesying. We insist that the prophet or presbytery has missed the mind of God.

This has happened a few times at our prophet seminars, where we provide a prophetic presbytery for those who attend. I remember in particular one minister who was unknown to most of those prophesying. No one said anything about his being a great prophet, nor much about even the attributes of a prophet. He came to me later complaining that the presbytery had missed it with him because they had not discerned his great call as a prophet of God.

This man approached me with an attitude of superiority. I had to counsel him through his hurt pride and resentment, dealing with him rather severely about his wrong spirit and attitude. He was not manifesting the wisdom that is from above.

Proper Attitude of a Truly Mature Person. The Bible says that if we rebuke a wise man, he will be wiser, and if we rebuke a fool, he will hate us. We want to be counted among the wise who can receive prophet rebuke and be made wiser. And that requires humility and meekness: *"The **humble** shall hear thereof and be glad"* (Ps. 34:2, emphasis added). *"Receive with **meekness** the engrafted word"* (James 1:21, emphasis added).

When Jesus prophesied to the seven churches of Asia in the Book of Revelation, He said: *"He that hath an ear, let him hear what the Spirit has to say."* It was not all complimentary. The words spoken to them required some adjustments in their attitudes and activities. The Lord told them that the proper response to the prophecy was repentance and submission, and there would be serious consequences if they responded otherwise.

Inaccurate Prophecy or Immature Person Responding. A mature person with the right attitude will respond to personal prophecy—even if it is corrective—with the attributes of heavenly wisdom: *"The wisdom that is from above is first pure, then peaceable, gentle, and easy to be entreated, full of mercy and good fruits, without partiality, and without hypocrisy"* (James 3:17). Other translations use words here like *teachable, open to reason, ready to be convinced, courteous, kind,* and *free from doubts, wavering,* and *insincerity.* A righteous and mature person will not respond with carnal or childish behavior even if a prophecy is inaccurate. How much more so, then, should we respond to a true personal prophecy with humility, meekness, and submission.

Pride Can Hinder Personal Prophecy From Coming to Pass. A good example of the need for humility in receiving

God's word to us is found in the story of Captain Naaman of Syria (2 Kings 5). He fell ill with leprosy, and wanted Elisha the prophet to heal him. When Elisha sent a messenger telling him to wash seven times in the river Jordan to be healed, he was outraged. His personal pride was hurt because Elisha had not come to him personally, and his sense of national pride was hurt because the Jordan was in Israel rather than Syria. In addition, the prophecy simply did not make sense to him. So he decided to go home angry.

Naaman would never have received his healing if his companion had not reasoned with him to put aside his pride and obey the Lord's word through Elisha. Having to dunk himself seven times in the muddy Jordan was humbling for Naaman; but when he disciplined himself to obey in detail, God's creative prophetic word was activated and germinated. It sprouted forth in full manifestation of the prophetic seed which had been planted by Elisha, and Naaman was healed.

Full, humble obedience automatically brings activation of the prophetic word. Nothing can stop the word from working once we have obeyed in every detail. We do not have to beg God to make it work, any more than a repenting sinner has to ask God to make sure His promise that the blood of Jesus cleanses from all sin will work when he believes and confesses Christ. Obedience to a prophecy activates it into fulfillment as surely as the right key turned in the ignition starts a car.

CHAPTER 18

HINDRANCES TO THE FULFILLMENT OF PERSONAL PROPHECY

We have already seen how the conditional nature of personal prophecy means that we must cooperate with God's word to us in order for it to be fulfilled. We have also examined the elements of a proper response. Now we must look more closely at what hinders personal prophecy from fulfillment, and the results of an improper response.

Basically, the same things that hinder us from appropriating the biblical promises also hinder us from appropriating and fulfilling our personal prophetic promises from the Lord. The Bible relates several incidents when people received a true word from a prophet or even directly from God Himself, yet they could not or would not accept the word as accurate or possible for their lives. The following problems are the most common hindrances illustrated in Scripture that can prevent us from accepting a prophecy, understanding it, relating to it, and receiving it in our spirit.

Unbelief

Unbelief is the number one hindrance to the fulfillment of personal prophecy. The Old and New Testament Scriptures verify this fact. Numbers chapters 13 and 14 relate the story of the children of Israel failing to fulfill their personal prophecy given to them by Moses. God had spoken a prophecy to them with His personal commitment to make it work. He demonstrated His desire to perform in His power. He worked miracles to get them out of Egypt and supernaturally met their every need for two years in their journey to the edge of their prophetically promised Canaan. Yet with all the proofs God had given them, they were still full of unbelief. *"So we see that they could not enter in because of unbelief"* (Heb. 3:19).

Unbelief dominates a person's life because of never coming to know God personally. The Israelites were ruled by their five senses and circumstances instead of God's prophetic promise. They looked at the problems instead of the prophecy; the walled cities instead of God's will; the giants instead of God's greatness; the natural impossibilities instead of the Almighty's personal promise. They were swayed by a negative report from ten of the twelve spies. They made their decision based on human reasoning and self-preservation rather than God's personal prophetic pledge to them. We must rise up in the spirit and resist and overcome all temptation to reason and doubt if we are to fulfill our personal prophecy from the Lord. Unbelief will definitely hinder anyone from obtaining the promises of the *Logos* or a personal *rhema*.

Mind-set

Most of us have preconceptions about life, about ourselves, and about theology; and when a prophetic word does not line up with our established thought patterns, we consider it unacceptable. We think we cannot relate to such a word, we may even resent it, and we tend to reject it altogether.

When Jesus began to speak prophetically about His death, burial, and resurrection, the disciples did not understand what He was saying. He seemed to be talking in riddles. Matthew tells us that Peter even grabbed Jesus by the shoulders and told Him not to talk like that. He resented and renounced such a prophetic declaration, because it did not agree with his personal goals and preconceptions about the Messiah (Matt. 16:21-22).

The Jews had a particular political mind-set about the coming of the Messiah. Any contrary prophetic word, even when it came from Jesus, was incomprehensible to them, and therefore unacceptable. So when Jesus spoke of a suffering, dying, resurrected Savior, it would not compute in their pre-programmed minds. Even the apostles shared the mind-set of their contemporaries, making it impossible for them to receive an immediate witness to and understanding of what was being prophesied.

Established Opinions Oppose True Prophecies. Today, we too may have a particular mind-set with regard to a way of life, a type of ministry, or a religious tradition. If so, we find it virtually impossible to receive a prophetic word contrary to our thinking and goals. Prophetic words of this nature are not understood until they actually come to pass. Only then do we understand at last and say, *"That's* what the prophet was talking about."

God speaks things of this nature so we will know after we have gone through it that it was in the mind and purpose of God all along, working out for our good and God's overall purpose and plan. It was only after Jesus suffered, died, and was resurrected that the disciples were ready to receive the true, literal application of the prophecy. The same prophetic word that had brought confusion and consternation to them when it was spoken became the word of greatest hope, encouragement, revelation, and consolation.

From the thousands of personal prophecies I have spoken to people over the last 35 years, I have received hundreds of testimonies verifying this prophetic principle. In 1981, for example, I preached and prophesied in a church in Atlanta, Georgia. I gave personal prophecies to over one hundred church staff leaders, including the bishop of the church.

Later the bishop testified that he had rejected a portion of his personal prophecy because of his mind-set at the time.

Just a week before I had come, he had told his staff that he would not be traveling abroad anymore so he could stay home and pastor the church. But a paragraph of his long prophecy stated that he would be traveling to the nations more than he had ever done before.

This word was rejected until two years later when he looked back over the time since the prophecy and realized that he had done exactly what the prophetic word had declared. Three years later, when I ministered in that church again, the bishop could affirm that the prophet was true and that his words had been accurate and had come to pass.

Problems With Prophetic Words Because of "Tenses." On another occasion I was prophesying over people in a church in Louisiana that emphasizes the importance of faith. The pastor had even written several books about positive confession and constant victory for the Christian who is walking in faith. I gave a long personal prophecy to this Christian man and his wife, and about half of it repeated themes like "Don't be discouraged...You are not at fault for what has happened... Your faith did not fail...I have not failed you...I am still in control...Don't blame yourself or try to understand or explain what has happened...Don't be confused or discouraged, but keep your confidence in God's wisdom and faithfulness."

After I was finished with this family and began to minister to others, the husband went back to our book and tape table to talk to my wife. He said he could not understand how the prophet could have missed it with him when he was so right on with all the others. He insisted that he was not discouraged, confused, or perplexed over anything; his faith was high and solid.

The problem was that the prophecy had been given in present tense, even though it actually applied to something in the future. (This is true of many Old Testament prophecies as well.) He was trying to understand an event that had not yet taken place. He was in chapter two of his life while the prophecy was referring to something in chapter three.

About a year later we received a letter from this same man telling us how the prophecy had become a blessing. His wife had been expecting a child, and they had been confessing a victorious birth and life for it. But the baby had been born dead. This event was catastrophic to them both emotionally and theologically, because they had no idea that something like this could possibly happen. (Only God knows why the baby did not live and I did not know the personal prophecy would be a comfort for such a time and situation.)

At that time, however, someone reminded them that their prophetic word had related to this very type of situation. So they took it out, typed it out, and meditated upon it. They discovered that the prophecy had described in detail the emotions and thoughts they were experiencing. So the prophecy brought great peace and consolation, releasing them from the pressure and the sense of condemnation the devil was heaping upon them.

Numerous other testimonies have been given to prophecies of this kind. Many have reported: "I didn't understand or relate to that part of the prophecy when you gave it, but now that I have gone through the experience, I fully understand and relate to what was spoken. Now I am greatly comforted in my spirit and mind."

No one can fully relate to a true word from the Lord that refers to a future situation, especially when it is contrary to our faith or mind-set. If a personal prophecy seems a little negative, or not according to our current thinking, we should still write it out, then wait and see. Like Jesus' prophecy of His suffering and resurrection, what seems now to be negative or confusing may become positive, enlightening, and encouraging in a future chapter of our life.

We should also remember that a false prophecy is one that will not come to pass. If it is not the word of the Lord, we do not have to be afraid of it, worry about it, or renounce it to keep it from happening. If it is the word of the Lord, then the time will come when what seemed like a negative word will show itself to be positive, productive, and profitable.

The Problem of Self-image

One particular form of preconception is especially powerful in hindering us from receiving and fulfilling personal prophecy: a wrong *self-image*. If we have a strong "failure complex" like the one Moses displayed at the burning bush, we will not be able to receive a word from God about how successful we can be (Exod. 3-4).

God spoke directly to Moses at the burning bush, accompanied with supernatural manifestations. Yet even the Almighty Himself could hardly convince Moses that the prophecy was true and could be fulfilled in his life. If such a word had come through a prophet instead of directly from God, he probably would not have even considered it.

Wrong Self-Opinions Sabotage Personal Prophecy. Even God Himself has a hard time convincing someone who has a low self-image and a failure complex. Sometimes we have sought like Moses to do the will of God and become God's "deliverer," but instead we have made a terrible mess of things, left the leadership ministry, and resolved to go to the back side of the desert, content with being a family man in a secular job. When that happens, God has to accompany the prophecy with supernatural anointing and manifestations in order for us to accept the prophecy as accurate and workable for us.

Reject the Fear of Rejection. If we have tried for years to make something happen, but nothing ever comes of it, then when the word of the Lord comes that it is finally going to happen, the soul defends itself by rejecting the prophecy. We do not want to be disappointed again, and we reason that things have never worked before, so why should they be any different now?

We must not develop a failure complex that hinders prophecy. We must guard our soul, heart, mind, and spirit with all diligence, pursuing our prophetic promise until it comes to pass. God is faithful to watch over His word to perform it.

Prophecy Pertains to the Impossible. If we focus our vision on the promise, rather than the time, the problems, or the contradicting evidence, we will find that man's impossibilities become God's opportunities. In fact, God's highest purpose and delight is to wait until man can see no possible way for His promise to be kept without supernatural intervention. That is why God waited till Sarah was past the natural bearing years to give her a son, and why Jesus waited until Lazarus had been dead for four days before arriving on the scene. Faith must be in God alone, not in the words but in the God who speaks them; not in our ability to appropriate, but in God's ability to accomplish His own prophesied purpose in our life.

Natural Resources and Scientific Logic Hindrances. Paul declared that the natural mind cannot comprehend the things of the Spirit because they are spiritually discerned. Sometimes simple human reasoning or scientific logic seems to insist that what God has promised is simply impossible and irrational. The scriptural examples of this kind of prophecy are numerous: the parting of the Red Sea (Exod. 14); the conquest of Jericho by marching and a shout (Josh. 6:1-20); the multiplication of oil (2 Kings 4:1-7); the change from a severe famine to abundance in a single day (2 Kings 6:24-33; 7:1-20). Personal prophecy is a "spiritual" function. It must be accepted in your spirit and acted upon with faith in God.

Soul Blockage

Sometimes it is not an idea or way of thinking that prevents us from believing a prophecy, but rather an emotion, a willful desire, or a personal ambition. This might be called a soul blockage, because the soul contains the *mind, will,* and *emotions* where these problems are located.

Emotions hinder us from believing, for example, when we fear man more than we fear God, seeking to please others more than Him. This was the problem of King Zedekiah (Jer. 38:19) and of Saul (1 Sam. 15:24). Our feelings also prevent us from faith when we have a personal dislike for the person giving the word, or a dislike for prophecy itself. This was the case with King Jehoram with regard to Micaiah (1 Kings 22:8), and King Zedekiah with regard to Jeremiah (Jer. 38:14-28).

Further reasons for unbelief include focusing on the problem instead of on the promise (Num. 13:30-31); a failure to come to know God personally (Dan. 11:32); or a motivation of self-preservation rather than God's glory (Rev. 12:11).

Impatience

Impatience is another major hindrance to fulfilling personal prophecy. The examples of this problem in Scripture are many. As we have seen, through impatience *Saul* not only hindered but actually voided the prophetic word he had received (1 Sam. 13:12). He impatiently "forced" himself to offer a sacrifice instead of waiting for Samuel to come as he had prophetically promised.

Moses also demonstrated impatience when he killed the Egyptian. He tried to fulfill his call as deliverer of his people before God had shown him the way. The result was that he was forced to flee to the desert and wait for 40 years until God opened the way and revealed the proper time.

Abraham and Sarah waited for ten years after they had entered Canaan, hoping that Abraham's personal prophecy of a son would come to pass. Sarah became impatient and decided not to wait any longer. She probably reasoned within herself that God had never told Abraham she had to be the child's mother. So she thought she could make the prophecy come to pass by giving her handmaiden Hagar to Abraham to become a surrogate mother.

Impatience Produces an "Ishmael" Ministry. *Abraham* did become a father, but the child was not the promised seed. The couple had not fulfilled God's will nor taken His way. So the result was Ishmael, who became a tormentor to the promised seed, Isaac. And Ishmael's descendants have continued to persecute the descendants of Isaac down to the present day.

Every time we fail to wait patiently until God reveals His divine way for prophesied ministry, an "Ishmael" ministry is born into the Church instead. Such a counterfeit ministry, produced our way instead of God's way, will be a thorn in the flesh of true ministry. So God's people must wait, and wait, and keep on waiting until God tells us clearly His divine way and appointed time for prophecy to be fulfilled.

Mary is a good example for us in this respect. She hid away in her heart her personal prophecy and meditated upon it while she waited over 33 years to see it fulfilled concerning her child, Jesus. Many things had to take place before she could see the fulfillment of the word that He would save His people from their sins. Jesus had to be killed, buried, and resurrected before He could cleanse us all by His blood.

Only God knows all the things that must happen before our personal prophecies can come to pass. Human impatience will only hinder. Instead, we must rest in faith, waiting patiently and leaning not to our own understanding. We must watch for God's way and take it one step at a time.

Negligence, Procrastination, and Slothfulness

The problems of negligence and procrastination add up to make slothfulness—another hindrance to the fulfillment of personal prophecy. Moses, for example, almost died at the hand of God before fulfilling his prophecy because he neglected to keep the Abrahamic covenant of circumcision for his sons. He was probably planning to do it, but never got around to it. His slothfulness in this matter almost cost him his life when God met him at an inn and sought to kill him (Exod. 4:24).

Putting off what God has told us to do can get us in serious trouble. Before I began writing my first book, *The Eternal Church*, I was stopped in my traveling ministry by an attack of kidney stones while I was in Atlanta, Georgia. I wondered, *How could this happen to me?* I had been miraculously healed of kidney stones three times before, since my first attack in 1963. So I was determined to be healed this time, too.

I went ahead ministering awhile despite the pain. But it intensified to the point that I had to be taken to the hospital. Blood tests there showed that an immediate operation was imperative. Though I cried to God to intervene supernaturally, and quoted all the Scriptures I knew about healing, nothing worked this time. All that came was a quiet assurance from God that it was all right to go ahead with the operation.

Principle of Recording and Reading Learned the Hard Way. I missed several important events, and my wife had to cancel several weeks of heavy itinerary. During this time the Lord impressed me to find all the recorded prophecies I had received since the first one in 1952, and write them out in chronological order in a notebook. To my surprise, one particular theme appeared again and again in prophetic words I had forgotten about. God had said many times to *write the book*, and to do it right away.

After reading one prophecy in particular that had said "the book!" seven times, I sought God to tell me the exact subject. I began research and writing, but once I was fully recovered the itinerary began to fill up again.

Just as I was getting ready to leave one day for a ministry trip, a good Christian friend called and came over for counsel. Upon arriving, she said: "God told me on the way over to your house that if you do not continue writing on the book, He will let your physical body be taken down again." I witnessed that it was God's word, cancelled the meetings, and kept on writing. During the next three years, in fact, I majored in writing and minored in itinerant meetings until the book was completely written and published—*The Eternal Church*.

Misapplication and Misinterpretation of Prophecy

Another problem that can hinder the fulfillment of personal prophecy is our tendency to misapply or misinterpret what we hear from God. Once again, Saul provides the classic biblical example of this hindrance. He manipulated his personal prophecy to please the people and himself by substituting sacrifice for obedience. God had told him to slaughter even the livestock of his conquered enemies, but instead he kept the best of the flocks and herds to offer as sacrifices to the Lord. Though the idea might sound religious and reasonable, he was actually using the captured livestock to save the people from having to slaughter their own on the altar.

Samuel declared in response to this disobedience that by God's standards, such a manipulation of prophecy for one's own purpose is the same as the sin of witchcraft; and to misinterpret the prophecy willfully and stubbornly for one's own interest is the same as idolatry. Thus Saul's behavior was counted as a trespass of iniquity against God Himself, even though the word had been spoken by the prophet in the name of the Lord.

Personal Prophecy Is No Plaything. The offense of taking prophecy too lightly, and not following it seriously, was no small thing with God. Jehovah sent the prophet to Saul to tell him that this failure to destroy utterly all that belonged to the Amalekites so frustrated God that He actually repented that He had ever given the kingship to Saul. The Lord consequently removed His anointing from Saul, and sent Samuel to anoint David king instead.

Ministers of the Gospel, and all the saints in the Church, should be assured that personal prophecy is nothing to play around with or take lightly. We cannot just assume as Saul did, "Well, the prophet doesn't understand the economics of the situation. The prophet is not a businessman, and besides— think how much this would please the congregation!"

Yes, what Saul and the soldiers did was much more logical, made better economic sense, and was more profitable to the people. It was even cloaked in the religious justification of sacrifice and worship to God. But all the human reasoning and business sense in the world will not excuse us from the sin of witchcraft and idolatry we commit when we manipulate personal prophecy to our own ends. God accepts no substitute for obedience, regardless of how pious or beneficial it may seem.

Pride

Pride is perhaps one of the most dangerous hindrances to the fulfillment of personal prophecy. Lucifer failed to fulfill his originally ordained ministry because of his pride. Isaiah tells us that he said in his heart, *"I will exalt my throne above the stars of God...I will ascend above the heights of the clouds, I will be like the Most High"* (Isa. 14:13-14). But the result was that he was thrown out of Heaven.

Evidently Saul also became proud, and it contributed to his downfall. Samuel referred to the time in the past when Saul used to be small in his own sight, implying that he now thought of himself as someone great (1 Sam. 15:17). Pride destroyed his ministry just as it had for lucifer.

Disappointment and Disillusionment

When things do not work out the way we want, our disappointment and disillusionment can hinder the fulfillment of God's word to us. Sarah is one biblical example of how these feelings can cause unbelief when we are given a prophecy. For 25 years after she had heard the prophetic word about bearing a son to Abraham, nothing had come of it. She had been disappointed 12 times in each of these years when her monthly cycle came around and proved that she was still not pregnant. Over three hundred times she had built up hopeful expectations, only to have her hopes dashed again and again.

Not surprisingly, when an angel appeared in Abraham's ninety-ninth year and said that a baby would be born to Sarah in nine months, her disillusionment said no. She laughed it off to keep from being disappointed again. The continual failure to produce a child had established in her a self-image of barrenness. All natural and soulish evidence overwhelmingly supported her conclusion that it was impossible for the prophetic word to be fulfilled in her case. God had seemingly waited too long. She and Abraham were both beyond the fertile years.

Nevertheless, Isaac was born. That fulfillment of prophecy should encourage us not to let our disappointment prevent us from believing the word of the Lord. We must be willing to wait despite apparent failure of the prophecy, and willing to go through God's process of procurement.

Blame Shifting, Self-Deception, and People Pleasing

Many a pastor, prophet, or other minister has failed to fulfill a personal prophecy or vision because they feared the deacons, the elders, the administrative board, or the congregation. They went by the vote of the people instead of by the voice of the Lord. Then, when things failed to turn out right, they blamed others for the problem.

Saul was guilty of this behavior in his disobedience toward his personal prophecy. "I feared the people," he said, "and obeyed their voice." His giving into fear and shifting of blame resulted in self-deception as well, for he insisted that he had obeyed God after all (1 Sam. 15:20-21).

Moses had a similar problem when he allowed his compassion for the people to make him determined that their generation would be the one to possess the promised land (Num. 14:11-21; 20:7-12). He eventually became angry with them in a way that caused him to disobey God. The final result was that neither they nor he received the promise of the Lord.

Results of an Improper Response

The results of an improper response to personal prophecy can be seen throughout the Scriptures. When Zacharias, for example, disbelieved the angel's word to him, he lost his speech for nine months. Moses' impatience, frustration, and resentment of God's people provoked him to act foolishly by striking the rock twice—and this one act cancelled his prophecy about entering the promised land. Over a million Israelite men and women died in the wilderness because of their rebellion despite God's prophecy to them. And King Zedekiah's improper response to Jeremiah's prophecies cost him his throne, his sight, and his freedom as he was carried off into bondage by his enemies.

An especially important example of improper response is that of King Joash of Israel, the grandson of Jehu (2 Kings 13:14-20). When Elisha was sick, Joash came to visit him, weeping over the prophet's terminal disease. Elisha then acted out a prophecy about the king's future accomplishments, and told Joash to get a bow and some arrows. Next he instructed the king to open an eastern window, put his hands on the bow, and shoot while Elisha put his own hands on the king's. Because Joash obeyed the prophet exactly, Elisha prophesied that he would have victory over the Syrians at Aphek.

Response to Prophet's Word Determines the Prophecy. Next, however, Elisha gave Joash a chance to act out of his own heart and spirit, in his own initiative. Much was riding on how he responded to Elisha's word. Elisha told the king to take up the other arrows and strike them on the floor, so he did so—three times. Then the prophet shouted angrily at the king: "You should have struck the floor five or six times, for then you would have beaten Syria until they were entirely destroyed. But now you will be victorious over Syria only three times."

Joash thus missed a golden opportunity because of his improper response to the word of the prophet. He could have obtained a full victory instead of a partial one. But his lack of zeal and determination diminished his prophetic potential.

An important principle is revealed in this story: We limit power and prophetic purpose by an improper response to the word of the prophet. If a man of God speaks to us in a role of prophet and tells us to do something, we should do it enthusiastically. Obedience can keep us from forfeiting our potential for powerful performance.

Four Types of Human Heart Soil

The results of the proper and improper response to personal prophecy can perhaps best be summed up by Jesus' parable of the sower (Matt. 13:3-9). He tells us that the human heart is like the ground, and each heart can be placed in one of four categories, according to how it responds to the word of God.

The *first type* of "heart soil" is that of the *wayside* or *sidewalk*. It lacks the ability to receive or retain the word. The *second type* is the *shallow, stoney ground*. It produces only a weak response to God's word, without a root to sustain it. This is the heart of the selfish people-pleaser.

The *third type* is the soil of *thorny mixture*. Though the soil is good, it is also worldly and materialistic. It has too many weeds, and so the response to God's word is eventually choked out.

Fourth and most important is the heart with *good ground*. It has been deeply plowed, constantly cultivated, and well watered. The heart of good soil has learned to discern the good seed from the bad, and it rejects the bad. This is the kind of soil we should all strive to have, so we can respond to the prophetic word of God with an abundant, hundredfold harvest.

CHAPTER 19

LIFE AND DEATH IN RELATION TO PERSONAL PROPHECY

We have received testimonies of Christians who have warred against the angel of death and won the battle because of their personal prophecy. One example is from a pastor in Florida whom I met in 1979 at a ministers' meeting. I preached for an hour and then prophesied over 25 pastors and their wives who were there. Since that time I have preached at this particular pastor's church in Ft. Walton Beach, Florida, on the average of twice a year. Because the Lord directed me years ago always to minister to the senior pastor and his family in each church where I visit, this pastor has received numerous prophecies.

In one of those prophecies, God spoke through the prophet a promise that he would be able to train his two sons in the ministry. At that time, neither one was inclined to the ministry; in fact, one of them was not very spiritually inclined at all. They were both at home and in their late teens at this time.

In June, 1981, this man's mother died of heart disease. A few hours later the same kind of heart attack hit him. Be enlightened by the following portion of Dr. L.M. Thorne's testimony:

That night the spirit of death left my mother and came on me. I really thought I was going to die. I believe I would have if my wife, my brother, and sister-in-law had not known how to fight a good warfare on my behalf. It felt as if I was out of my body looking down on it. I felt I had somehow been separated from it.

I was putting up no personal resistance to this intense warfare by my family when the Holy Spirit brought to me some prophecies Dr. Bill Hamon had given over me concerning the ministry. He had said that I would be in the ministry with my two sons one day. I fully trust Dr. Hamon's words. He has a great track record at our church, so I trusted him as a prophet of God.

When the Holy Spirit brought these prophecies to me, I thought, satan, you can't kill me; I have not fulfilled these prophecies yet. So at that time I began to fight a good warfare on my own and almost instantly I began to get better. Up to that time I was just holding my own. My family was keeping me alive but I had to get into the battle. As soon as I did, I began to get better. I began to fight according to First Timothy 1:18.

Needless to say, I won. That was six years ago, and I am still healthy. Personal prophecy is a mighty weapon to use to defeat the enemy when he attacks you. Fight the good fight of faith with those prophecies that have gone over you.

This minister of God warred a warfare against the untimely arrival of the angel of death and won because he believed and acted upon his personal prophecies. He is a strong believer in the doctrine of divine healing, but it was not just a *Logos* Word that sparked his faith, but a *rhema* word from a prophet.

Paul told Timothy to war a good warfare and fight the good fight of faith, with the personal prophecies that had gone over him. The apostle instructed Timothy to study the Scriptures and preach the word (*Logos*), but he also charged him to war a personal warfare according to the personal prophecies (*rhema* word) which the apostle Paul and prophet Silas and other ministers had given to him at various times, including his ordination. He was given spiritual gifts and ministry by prophecy with the laying on of hands. And he was to meditate upon these prophecies and give himself wholly to them (1 Tim. 1:18; 4:14-15).

The Dead Raised

Our good friends, Roz and Syl Sozio, had a similar experience in the beginnings of their life together. They have driven over eight hundred miles round trip each time to attend more than a dozen of the CI seminars, and they are now conducting the same type of Holy Spirit and prophet seminars around the country, as well as fulfilling their local church ministry. But this would never have happened in their lives if it had not been for a personal prophecy which Roz had received that activated her faith to believe for the dead to be raised.

Their complete testimony will soon be published, but just the end result will be told here to show the power of the prophetic word. On June 19, 1980, Syl passed out in their apartment. The paramedics were called, they worked with him for 45 minutes, and he was pronounced clinically dead. No heartbeat or blood pressure reading could be found. While they were unhooking their equipment, Roz was quickened and challenged by the word of the Lord she had received. She prayed the prayer of faith and rebuked the spirit of death, and to the astonishment of the paramedics he came alive. A miracle took place because Roz acted upon her *rhema* from the Lord.

Faith comes and works when we know we have received a rhema from the Lord. Great men of God such as Smith Wigglesworth raised many from death by the working of miracles and the gift of faith. If we read their testimonies closely, however, we find that they first received a word from the Lord concerning when, where, and how to pray the prayer of faith. The *Logos* is the launching pad and structure for all authority, but it is the *rhema* that ignites the fuel and gives thrust for launching any rocket of accomplishment with God.

Prophecy From a *Rhema*, Not the *Logos*

The root problems with personal prophecy in relation to victory over death are the same as those relating to victory over sickness and disease. The death, burial, and resurrection of Jesus Christ provided victory over sin, sickness, and death. Eternal spiritual life and physical immortality are part of the gospel the same as salvation, water baptism, healing, the gift of the Holy Spirit, and other New Testament truths. Jesus arose victorious with the keys of death, hell, and the grave: *"Jesus Christ **hath abolished death, and hath brought life and immortality** to light through the gospel"* (2 Tim. 1:10, emphasis added).

We have the same scriptural proof that Christ Jesus obtained victory over death for every Christian as we have for His victory over sin and sickness. But when personal prophecy is given from head knowledge of scriptural truth and not from a *rhema* in the heart, it rarely comes to pass. Fact functions in the head, but faith flows from the heart.

Jesus Gained Victory Over All Things. Jesus has overcome death for every Christian, but there has not been one report in almost two thousand years of Christianity that even one saint has gone to Heaven to stay without dying. Death passed upon all men because of Adam's sin, but Jesus has redeemed us from the curse of death and broken the appointment with death. The Bible declares that this *Logos* truth will someday become a *rhema* reality, and *"we shall not die, but we shall be changed in a moment in the twinkling of an eye,"* *"for mortality shall be swallowed up of* [Christ's] *life"* (2 Cor. 5:4; 1 Cor. 15:52; 2 Tim. 1:10).

Until God manifests immortality in the physical bodies of the saints, we all will have to die sometime by some means. Disease, sickness, accidents, and old age are all agents of death. We can overcome many of his agents, but eventually one of them will be used to finish our mortal life and ministry on earth.

Our ultimate battle is not with sickness, disease, and calamities, but with death itself. Death is the enemy and robber of mortal life. That is why the Scripture declares that death is the last enemy to be destroyed by the Church (1 Cor. 15:26).

The *Logos* tells us it is God's will that we have immortality and live forever; the *rhema* lets us know whether it is God's will for a person to die at this time or whether it is the devil trying to rob him or her of life prematurely. Just because people have lived the allotted 70 years does not mean that it is automatically God's will for them to die when one of death's agents attack them. The place of wisdom is to take the stand that it is always God's will to save the soul, heal the body, and deliver from death. We must believe, confess, and declare it. But we must not speak it as a "thus saith the Lord" in a personal prophecy to a particular person and situation unless we are absolutely positive that we have received a Holy Spirit-inspired *rhema* from God.

Presumptuous Personal Prophecy. I have heard of some extreme cases of presumptuous personal prophecy and rhema in this regard. The followers of the greatest prophet of the Church in the late '40s to early '60s developed a few fanatic followers during the last few years of his ministry. When he died, these followers were determined that God was going to raise him from the dead. They held his body out for months, believing, prophesying, and decreeing that he would be raised from the dead on Easter morning. But they were finally forced legally to bury him.

I also heard of a self-proclaimed, charismatic prophetess in Phoenix, Arizona. Her father died, and she had prophesied that he would not. So when he did die, she prophesied that he would be raised from the dead. She kept him in her home, packed in ice, waiting for his resurrection, until the authorities ordered her to bury him. She then placed him in a van packed in ice and ran from the law for three months, determinedly prophesying that he would be raised. The law finally caught up with her and forced her to bury her father's body.

Some years ago numerous people died prematurely in the Midwest among a group who strongly believed in the biblical truth of divine healing. They became anti-medicine and refused all natural help from doctors. In doing so, they tried to make people fulfill the *Logos* without a *rhema* of faith and revelation by the Spirit. The result was that they made a truth into a tragedy; a reality into a religion of rigid rules; a faith into a formula. They moved from being directed by the Spirit to being dominated by doctrine; from being motivated by faith to obtain to being motivated by fear of failure to obey; from inward motivation to outward, corporate conformity.

Proper Use of *Logos* and *Rhema*—Personal Prophecy and Faith Declarations. Any time man takes a spiritual truth and tries to make it work without the Spirit of God, it becomes a "form of godliness" without the life-giving force that makes it a workable reality. *"The letter killeth, but the Spirit giveth life"* (2 Cor. 3:6b). Trying to make the *Logos* work without a *rhema* is like trying to make a car function without fuel, or trying to make the fuel fulfill its purpose without spark plugs to ignite it into powerful performance. But fuel ignited without being contained and directed properly becomes a destructive force. We need the Bible, but we also need the Holy Spirit to bring illumination and inspiration for the proper application and performance of God's Word.

CHAPTER 20

PROPHETIC CONCLUSION AND CHARGE

After reading this volume you should have reached the conclusion that our God is a talking heavenly Father who earnestly desires to communicate with His children on earth. We saw in Scripture that prophets and prophecy have always been Heaven's main channels for broadcasting the thoughts of God to mankind. True prophecy is simply God talking to us. With this definition, we can truly say that prophecy is an eternal attribute of Almighty God. Prophecy was manifested in the garden of Eden before man fell. God walked in the garden and talked (prophesied) to Adam and Eve, and Adam prophesied to his wife that she would be the mother of all living. We find in the Book of Revelation that God is still "talking" to mankind after the establishment of the new heavens and new earth. Prophets and prophecy are mentioned six times in the last chapter of the Bible (Rev. 22).

Different Prophetic Realms. We discovered that there are numerous prophetic realms, the greatest being the prophecy of Scripture, which is called the *Logos*, the Bible, the Word of God. Biblical prophecies are separated into two categories, unconditional/general prophecies and conditional/personal prophecies. The unconditional/general prophecies are the

Logos Scriptures that reveal the nature, character, and purposes of God. They are decrees of God that will come to pass at some time and place with some people. They cannot fail.

The conditional/personal prophecies are words that God has spoken to people throughout the Bible and even in this present day. These are prophetic *rhema* words that can fail because of man's improper response. Personal prophecy is not a side issue, but is in the main stream of God's activities. *There are more illustrations of personal prophecy in the Bible than any other subject.*

Only Ministry Commanded to Covet. The prophetic ministry is the only one that Scripture commands us to covet. *"Covet to prophesy"* (1 Cor. 14:39b). We are to make *love* our goal and *"desire spiritual gifts, but rather that ye may prophesy"* (1 Cor. 14:1b). Prophecy is representative of all the manifestations (gifts) of the Holy Spirit which reveal God's desires by speaking, revealing, and healing.

Personal Prophecy Part of God's Plans. Personal prophecy is not to dominate a person's life, but it can play a vital part in helping people to understand and fulfill the will of God. The stop-and-go lights of the divine *Word, will* and *way* are the surest methods of walking and working in harmony with Heaven. Personal prophecy is like any powerful force such as water, wind, or a laser beam. If properly directed, it produces much good, but if wrongly directed, it can do much damage.

Prophets Disciplined and Prophecy Directed. Though prophets are an ascension gift of Christ and personal prophecy is a divine operation of the Holy Spirit, yet there are divine disciplines and proper procedures to follow. Prophecy is a spirit manifestation subject to the prophet (1 Cor. 14:32). There are guidelines that need to be followed and proper responses that need to be made for prophecy to become productive and unfailing. These guidelines have been amplified within this volume by showing personal prophecy in relation to every major area of life from having babies to life and death.

The Prophets Are Coming! Finally, we discovered that God is raising up a company of prophets in these last days. They will prepare the way for Christ's second coming as John the Baptist prepared the way for Christ's first coming. They will prepare the way by bringing illumination upon Scriptures which the Holy Spirit has been commissioned to restore and activate within the Church. There is no way for Jesus to return from Heaven until all Scriptures spoken by the prophets have been fulfilled. Jesus is held in the heavens until... (Acts 3:21).

God's Purpose for Prophets. The prophets are anointed to "make ready a people" purified and perfected for God's eternal purpose. Prophets are not only to preach the *Logos*, but to minister a *rhema* to people. They are New Testament ministers who can minister the Spirit of God as easily as they minister the Word of God (2 Cor. 3:6).

Prophets have the special call and anointing to activate spirituality, spirit sensitivity, and spiritual gifts within the saints. *Prophets* can activate gifts of the Spirit within the saints the same way an *evangelist* can activate the gift of eternal life within sinners. An evangelist preaches the word of truth concerning salvation, then asks for a proper response of coming forward and repeating the sinner's prayer. He then declares to those who responded that they have the gift of eternal life.

Word of God and Holy Spirit Our Only Proof. Evaluate how you came to your present status. Have you been born again, born from above, birthed into the Kingdom by the Spirit of God? Do you know that you are a child of God? How do you know that you are a true child of God and not just a convert to a religious faith? There are only two ways to know beyond a shadow of a doubt: 1) *Word of God* knowledge from the *Logos*, 2) the *Holy Spirit* witness from the rhema. John said, *"These things have I **written** unto you that believe...that ye may **know**..."* (1 John 5:13, emphasis added). Paul said, *"The* [Holy] *Spirit beareth witness with **our spirit**, that we are the children of God"* (Rom. 8:16, emphasis added).

Faith Knowledge vs. Natural Understanding. When we're in the right place doing the right thing, and hearing and speaking the right words, the Spirit will bear witness to God's will and way. Words are not the only form of communication; the Spirit has a language of its own that allows us to know in a way not based on natural understanding. Because faith is an attribute of the Spirit, our redeemed spirit can know with full assurance long before understanding can perceive.

Learning the Language of Our Redeemed Spirit. This is the day and hour when Christians must learn the language of the Spirit so they can comprehend with understanding what the Spirit is trying to communicate with its wordless language. For that reason, our organization—Christian International—conducts "Schools of the Holy Spirit" to teach saints how to discern between their soulish realm and their spirit realm. Only the Holy Spirit can illuminate the Word of God and separate between soul and spirit (Heb. 4:12). So the saints need to allow the Holy Spirit and the Word to operate in them, exercising their spiritual senses.

Saints must have training in these matters, so we have what we call "Spiritual Exercise Training Sessions." Paul declared this need emphatically in his discourse on going on to maturity: *"Strong meat belongeth to them that are of full age, even those who by **reason of use** have their **senses exercised to discern** both **good** and **evil**"* (Heb. 5:12-6:3, emphasis added). This must be more than biblical knowledge for the head; it involves spiritual senses rightly developed to discern and witness to the Spirit.

Prophets Seminars and Conferences. I conduct prophets seminars at Christian International and prophets conferences in churches throughout the world to clarify, amplify, and magnify the office of the prophet. Prophetic presbytery is made available to all who attend the CI seminars to give them the benefits of personal prophecy. The prophets seminars are designed to educate and activate those who are called to the prophetic ministry. However, this worldwide end-time revival will not be accomplished by just a few preachers, but the "***saints****...shall take the kingdom*" (Dan. 7:18,27, emphasis added).

Training Saints to Rule and Reign. In these days God is raising up, not just a company of prophets with spiritual perception, but also a company of overcoming believers. They will become the jewels in God's crown and return with Him to discern between the righteous and the wicked (Mal. 3:16-4:3). They will sit with Christ on His throne of judgment when He separates the sheep nations from the goat nations; and they will rule those nations with a rod of iron. They will be able to discern righteously and execute God's judgments in righteousness (Rev. 2:26-27; Matt. 25:31-33; Ps. 149:6-9).

Time for Perfecting—Not Preserving. I believe it is time for the fivefold ministers of God to fulfill their ordained commission of perfecting, equipping, and maturing the saints. Pastors must unlock the nursery where they have their saints hidden away to keep them innocent and preserved. For God never said to preserve the saints, but rather to perfect the saints, to bring them to *maturity* as well as *purity*, to make them productive while making sure they are protected.

The saints must be educated, exposed, and exercised in mature spiritual discernment—not encouraged to escape. Ministers must get them out of the dark closet of an unhealthy protectionist mentality so they can be exposed to the light of spiritual sensitivity and maturity. Pastors and teachers can no longer afford to feed the saints just the milk of the Word; they must begin giving them strong meat in teaching and opportunities to exercise their spiritual senses until they learn to discern for themselves. *"Whom shall He teach knowledge? and whom shall He make to understand doctrine? them that are weaned from the milk, and drawn from the breasts"* (Isa. 28:9). God's main purpose of the fivefold ministry to the saints is for their "Maturing for Ministry, Training for Reigning, and Schooling for Ruling" (Eph. 4:11-15).

Spiritual Maturity—A Priority. The saints must learn how to discern and witness to what is doctrinally true. But they must also learn to discern between the *spirit* of truth and the *spirit* of error, between true prophecies and false prophecies, between true ministers and false ministers. They must be able to discern between their own soul and spirit so they can be led by the Spirit and recognize when the Holy Spirit is bearing witness to their spirit. Christian maturity and spiritual sensitivity are no longer an option. They are an absolute necessity for those who would be overcomers in these last days.

Books and CDs Series by Dr. Bill and Evelyn Hamon

Books by Dr. Bill Hamon

Prophetic Scriptures Yet to be Fulfilled - 3rd Reformation
The Day of the Saints
Who Am I and Why Am I Here
Apostles Prophets and the Coming Moves of God
Prophets and Personal Prophecy
Prophets and the Prophetic Movement
Prophets Pitfalls and Principles
Birthing God's Purpose
Prophetic Destiny and the Apostolic Reformation
Fulfilling Your Personal Prophecy
The Eternal Church
The Eternal Church Hardback

Books by Evelyn Hamon and Jane Hamon

Divine Flexibility (Evelyn Hamon)
The Spiritual Seasons of Life (Evelyn Hamon)
God's Tests are Positive (Evelyn Hamon)
Dreams and Visions (Jane Hamon)
The Deborah Company (Jane Hamon)
The Cyrus Decree (Jane Hamon)

CD Series, Tape Sets and Audio Books

Who Am I and Why Am I Here Audio Book CD (Dramatized Voices)
Prophetic Activation (Dr. Bill Hamon)
The Restoration and Destination of The Church (Dr. Bill Hamon)
The Saints Movement (Dr. Bill Hamon)
Prophetic Pitfalls (Dr. Bill Hamon)
The 10 M's (Dr. Bill Hamon)
Dealing with Life's Challenges Tape Set (Evelyn Hamon)
Handling Life's Realities Tape Set (Evelyn Hamon)

To Order these or other products:

Online orders: www.ChristianInternational.org
or Write: Call: 1-800-388-5308
Christian International Ministries Network   Fax: 850-231-1485
PO Box 9000   Email: lionking@cimn.net
Santa Rosa Beach, FL 32459

In the right hands This Book will Change Lives!

Most of the people that need this message will not be looking for this book. To change their life you need to put a copy of this book in their hands.

> *But others (seeds) fell into good ground, and brought forth fruit, some a hundred-fold, some sixty-fold, some thirty-fold* (Matt. 13:3-8).

Our ministry is constantly seeking methods to find the good ground, the people that need this anointed message to change their life. Will you help us reach these people?

> *Remember this—a farmer who plants only a few seeds will get a small crop. But the one who plants generously will get a generous crop* (2 Cor. 9:6).

EXTEND THIS MINISTRY BY SOWING
3-BOOKS, 5-BOOKS, 10-BOOKS, **OR MORE TODAY,**
AND BECOME A LIFE CHANGER!

Thank you,

Don Nori Sr., Publisher
Destiny Image
Since 1982

DESTINY IMAGE PUBLISHERS, INC.

*"Speaking to the Purposes of God for This Generation
and for the Generations to Come."*

VISIT OUR NEW SITE HOME AT
WWW.DESTINYIMAGE.COM

FREE SUBSCRIPTION TO DI NEWSLETTER

Receive free unpublished articles by top DI authors, exclusive

discounts, and free downloads from our best and newest books.

Visit www.destinyimage.com to subscribe.

Write to: Destiny Image
              P.O. Box 310
              Shippensburg, PA 17257-0310

Call: 1-800-722-6774

Email: orders@destinyimage.com

For a complete list of our titles or to place an order
online, visit www.destinyimage.com.

FIND US ON FACEBOOK OR FOLLOW US ON TWITTER.

www.facebook.com/destinyimage   facebook
www.twitter.com/destinyimage   twitter